BATH  BED
12X19

BED
12X19

STUDY
12X16

BED
12X19

BED
16X19

BATH

ED
X19

CL

CL

CL

FOYER

STUDY
19X13

BATH

OY

CL

BATH  CL

BATH

AIR
SHAFT

BATH

CL  CL

PANTRY

DINING
24X18

16

BATH

FOYER

LIVING
18X20

NG
18

OFF.

CL

CL

15

CL

DINING
24X20

FAMILY
10X15

CL

BED
24X15

LIBRARY
18X10

17S

LAUN

CL  CL

KITCHEN
20X12

17S

16

KITCHEN
20X12

BATH

BED
18X12

KIT.
11X20

DN TO BSMT

BATH

CLOS.
18X9

BATH

COURTYARD

BATH

CL

BED
18X21

12

CL

BED
13X13

KITCHEN
16X12

BATH

BATH

OFFICE
20X27

7

CL

LIVING
24X15

DN TO
BSMT

BED
18X13

CL

DINING
9X12

12

FICE
X17

STOR.

CL

KIT.

OFFICE

CL

AIR
SHAFT

BATH

DN TO BSMT

KITCHEN

LIVING
24X18

14

CL

FOYER

LIVING
18X16

BATH

7

CL

8

KIT.

CL

KITCHEN
16X9

10

BATH  CL

KIT.  1/2B

9

DN TO BSMT

BATH

BED
14X12

TUDY
5X24

LIVING
19X21

LIBRARY
15X18

LIVING/DINING
29X24

LIVING
19X21

LIBRARY
22X15

DINING
16X12

DN TO BSMT

# THE DAKOTA

# The Dakota
## A History of the World's Best-Known Apartment Building

by ANDREW ALPERN

with contributions by CHRISTOPHER S. GRAY
and photographs by KENNETH G. GRANT

PRINCETON ARCHITECTURAL PRESS

NEW YORK

2015

FRONTISPIECE: In this image from 2014, at the left is the white brick Mayfair Tower apartment house at 15 West 72 Street, built following the sale of the Dakota to the tenants' co-op corporation and the sale of the adjoining parking lot to a developer. The period replica street lights evident in the photograph are at least the fourth set to have been installed along Central Park West. The flagpole was an early addition in the 19th century. *Kenneth Grant*

Library of Congress Cataloging-in-Publication Data available upon request from the publisher

Published by
Princeton Architectural Press
37 East 7th Street, New York, New York 10003
*www.papress.com | blog.papress.com*

ISBN 978-1-61689-437-5

Floor plans by Mia Ho

❁

AUTHOR'S NOTE: A diligent search was made to find the current holders of the intellectual property rights of all previously-published or otherwise-copyrighted material. Where no rightsholder could be found, a suitable credit line has been provided wherever possible. Appropriate amends and notation will be made in future editions to the extent owners of un-credited rights come forward. Correction of any errors (with documentation or suitable citation) will be welcomed and will be reflected in future editions. Please address the author in care of the publisher.

MANUFACTURED IN THE UNITED STATES OF AMERICA

# CONTENTS

# PREFACE

$\mathcal{A}$PARTMENT HOUSES and office buildings have been the defining architectural elements of New York since the late 19th century. Office towers have gone higher and higher, with aggressive public-relations battles being fought again and again over which developer can win the bragging rights for the tallest. Only recently have newly-constructed apartment towers begun to challenge the elevated offices for pieces of the sky. But until not very long ago, the measuring stick for apartments was luxury alone. Luxury of space, of grandeur, of intricacy and ornament, of privacy, and of amenity. How those words have been defined has changed over time, and which buildings qualify for entry into the Pantheon of Luxe is sometimes arguable, but one apartment building was destined from its inception to epitomize the experience of luxury living. From the very first published notices telling of Edward Clark's intention to build a truly grand multiple dwelling in the newly-developing Upper West Side, the descriptions all told of luxury on a scale never-before attempted. Clark's project was the pioneer, and was unquestionably the first truly luxury apartment building in New York. In size and significance, it was the top of the mountain. Architect Henry J. Hardenbergh set the standard, but of course his accomplishment merely set the ball rolling. After all, this is New York, where every record is made to be broken and every achievement improved upon. The early 20th century architects Rosario Candela and James E. R. Carpenter redefined and redirected upper-class housing to reflect changes in living styles of wealthy New Yorkers from those who first occupied the Dakota's sprawling apartments. And predictably, the planning and design principles that helped to mould apartments at the upper echelons of the city's dwellings trickled down to those intended for the middle classes as well. New York was and is a city of apartments at all levels, and the top of the mountain is now a broad plateau shared by many apartment buildings. Some are aloof refined aristocrats of great age; some are sleekly chic and timeless; some crisply and newly-minted. But standing proud, polished, and protected is the Dakota, distinctive and instantly recognizable.

As with all of my prior books, this one happened quite by chance. An emailed inquiry from someone I didn't know piqued my interest. Scott Cardinal had some questions about the Dakota that went beyond what I had said about the building in two of my previous apartment house books. When he came up to New York some weeks later, we met. I had prepared a packet of photocopies of material from my files to give him, but in doing so I reread tattered old articles and reacquainted myself with the building's history. Scott's enthusiasm was infectious, and with his encouragement I decided to put the story together as a book. I enlisted the help of architect Mia Ho to create readable and reasonably accurate floor plans of the building using a disparate accumulation of ancient rental plans, individual apartment layouts, and alteration drawings gleaned from many different sources. The doyen of New York's buildings, architectural historian Christopher Gray, is an old friend who very kindly allowed me to mine the many relevant articles he had written in the past. Much of the vivid descriptive material in the text owes its existence to Christopher's decades of research and writing. Ken Grant is the quintessential New Yorker who tirelessly walks the city's streets with superb photographic equipment slung around his neck, recording the buildings of the city (and coming back repeatedly to re-record when the street is free from cars or snow or a surfeit of intrusive delivery people). Ken produced a magnificent digital visual record of the Dakota, from which a selection of images appears here. Michael Garrett augmented Ken's photographs with others to help tell the story, as well as providing support, encouragement, and wise advice whenever needed. Those people (and quite a few others, who know who they are) have helped immeasurably in the preparation and production of this book. They have my very heart-felt thanks and appreciation. There are doubtless errors on these pages nonetheless, and those are mine alone. But if the reader will ignore any shortcomings of the book, an entertaining and informative trip into the past should be the result. That is certainly the intention.

ANDREW ALPERN
*June 2015*

FIG. 1. Pencil drawing of the Dakota entrance by Richard Britell, *richardbritell.blogspot.com*

# CHAPTER 1

# Apartment Houses: historically and around the time of the Dakota

T HE DAKOTA is the Dowager Queen Mother of apartment houses, the first to sit on America's residential throne, and the *primus inter pares* of the aristocracy of multiple-dwellings. It is the measuring stick for all subsequent efforts and still enjoys superior status in the hierarchy of housing for the well-heeled, its apartments commanding prices that often warrant headline attention in the media. The Dakota was the first truly luxury apartment house in New York, and more than 130 years later it remains among the finest and most desirable places to live in the city.

We take apartment houses for granted, and for the vast majority of New Yorkers (at least those in Manhattan), an apartment of some sort is the assumed and only practical form of available housing. Yes, there are one-family row-houses still (or again) occupied by a single family, and even a scattering of grand private mansions, but New York's central borough is emphatically an apartment enclave. The outer boroughs are only partially different. In many ways they are mini-Manhattans with mid-rise and high-rise apartment buildings, but large sections resemble suburban towns, with tree-lined streets of free-standing one-family wood or brick houses. But when the Dakota was built, those boroughs weren't part of New York City. By the time the five-borough metropolis that we now know as New York was created in 1898, apartment-house living was well on its way to being the primary form of housing for both financial and practical physical reasons.

When apartments were first introduced for those who were more prosperous than the laboring classes and considered themselves higher on the social scale, they were met with resistance. In New York, living in a set of rooms with others above or below you meant living in a tenement, and tenements were for poor people, disreputable people, the lower classes. Although this was the prevailing view in all of America, it was not the case in Europe. Tenements had existed as early as ancient Rome, where they were cheaply constructed for the lowest classes and were frequently subject to conflagration or structural collapse. Apartment buildings five and six stories high for the middle classes emerged in Scotland in the 17th century, and by the 18th century they had attained in both England and the Continent a level of sophistication sufficient to make them acceptable for persons of quality.

In France, the 18th and 19th centuries saw apartment houses achieve elegance, architectural distinction, and wide acceptance as an affordable and practical mode of living. The French version

FIG. 2. The Stuyvesant, 142 East 18 Street
*Arnold Moses, 1936*

FIG. 3. The Stuyvesant, entrance detail
*Arnold Moses, 1936*

also contributed to the social stability as well. In that country one could find a mix of social classes within the same building, in a reverse hierarchy. Those *highest* on the economic and social scale were on the *lowest* floors, with the income levels and social status of the tenants declining with each successive flight of stairs that had to be climbed to reach the housing provided. By the middle of the 19th century, Paris and other French cities were dense with these apartment houses.

Eventually, the concept of a multiple-dwelling that was not a tenement reached these shores. The Stuyvesant Apartments of 1869, designed by Richard Morris Hunt and built by Rutherfurd Stuyvesant at 142 East 18 Street, is generally acknowledged to have been the first multi-family dwelling house designed for people who would live at a qualitatively different level from those inhabiting tenement apartments (figs. 2 and 3). It offered clearly defined living and dining rooms, separate from the bedrooms, treated the kitchen as a service space, and included a separate service stair and a sleeping room for a domestic servant. Collectively, these elements represented a clear departure from prior tenements, and their provision in a socially-acceptable building created a new residential market (fig. 56 on page 42).

During the 1870s, many developers experimented with the new building type. Two that remain of that first cohort are 21 East 21 Street designed by Bruce Price, and 129 East 17 Street, designed by Napoleon LeBrun (figs. 4 and 5). Each originally had one apartment per floor, the 21st Street building with a small elevator, the 17 Street one without. The 21st Street units were subdivided many years ago, but when the 17th Street one was converted to a cooperative, units were combined, so there is now a triplex, a duplex, and two simplexes, including the unit on the roof that was an early addition for a janitor. Some of the initiatives of that period were much more ambitious than these two, although none remains.

The Albany, on the west side of Broadway from 51st to 52nd Streets, was designed by John Babcock and completed in 1876 (fig. 6). With entrances to its apartments on the two side streets, the entire ground floor along Broadway was devoted to stores. Upstairs, there were ten apartments per floor (fig. 57 on page 42).

The apartments in The Albany were evidently planned for a class of householders who were willing to live on less-than-upper-class Broadway, and who would not be put off by cramped room sizes and by dining rooms and kitchens that opened onto small interior air shafts.

The first apartment house named the Osborne (fig. 7, and fig. 58 on page 42) was designed to attract the sort of residents to whom the Dakota would later aspire. It was constructed on the east side of Fifth Avenue, mid-block between 52nd and 53rd Streets, immediately adjoining the grand mansion of its developer on the corner of 52nd Street across from the mansion that now houses Cartier, the jeweler. Unlike most real estate developers and operators of the time, this one was a woman, Anna Lohman. And not just any rich woman, but the infamous and socially-shunned abortionist who called herself Madame Restell.

This Osborne was completed in 1876 by architects Duggin & Crossman, who were specialists in top-end speculative row houses. Staying in character, they designed a comparable apartment house looking just like two overblown side-by-side brownstones, except for the single central doorway and ornate porch with elaborate torchères to light the entrance.

Around the same time that the Dakota was being constructed in the far-off Upper West Side, other apartment houses were being built in parts of the city that were already well developed. Some even appeared to approach the size or the grandeur of what the Dakota's architect Henry Hardenbergh had designed, but for one reason or another, none achieved the top billing that the Dakota garnered even before it had opened, and none commanded the rent levels that the Dakota did.

FIG. 5. 129 East 17 Street

FIG. 4. 21 East 21 Street

FIG. 6.
The Albany,
the west side
of Broadway,
51st Street to
52nd Street

The Manhattan, at 244 East 86 Street (fig. 8) was designed by Charles Clinton and built in 1880 by the members of the Rhinelander family. It was aimed at a middle-class market, notwithstanding that it was adjacent to the elevated railway along Second Avenue. Robert F. Wagner Sr. (first a New York State senator and later a United States senator) raised his family there, includ-

FIG. 7. The original Osborne of 1876, Fifth Avenue between 52nd and 53rd Streets
*Carpentry and Building, January 1880*

ing his namesake son, who later went on to become Mayor of New York City The Manhattan's apartments were subdivided during the 1930s and 1940s, but later were reconstructed as small luxury apartments when the building's lot was merged with adjoining property and its unbuilt zoning capacity was shifted to enable a large new tower to be built next to it.

On 31 August 1881, less than a year after the building of the Dakota was begun, The Windermere opened. Actually three buildings built together to look as if they were one, this complex is at the southwest corner of 57th Street and Ninth Avenue (fig. 9). The architects were Nathanial A. McBride and Theophilus G. Smith. It was aimed at a middle-class market, as was the Manhattan, and also adjoined an elevated railway (along Ninth Avenue). As originally constructed, there were 39 apartments in all, of seven and eight rooms. While this may sound spaciously luxurious, the architectural planning was primitive, re-

FIG. 8. The Manhattan, built in 1880 at the southwest corner of 86th Street and Second Avenue, was the first uptown project of the Rhinelander family. This image dates to circa 1944, after the elevated railway tracks had been removed and after the subdivision of the original apartments, which had necessitated the addition of exterior fire escapes. *Office for Metropolitan History*

FIG. 9. The Windermere, 400, 404, and 406 West 57 Street at the southwest corner of Ninth Avenue, showing a bit of the elevated railway tracks, about 1939. *Municipal Archives, City of New York*

FIG. 10. The Chelsea, 222 West 23 Street

sulting in something better perhaps than tenement planning but not luxurious (fig. 60 on page 44).

What is now the Hotel Chelsea at 222 West 23 Street (fig. 10) began life in 1883 as an early version of a cooperative apartment house (fig. 59 on page 43). It was a semi-socialistic venture of Philip Gengembre Hubert, a French architect born in 1830 who came to New York and went into partnership with James Pirsson as the firm of Hubert Pirsson & Company (later Hubert, Pirsson & Hoddick). Hubert and Pirsson initially built a practice of small buildings in the neo-Gothic style, including what is now the picturesque little Church of St. Thomas More, built in 1870 at 65 East 89 Street. In 1880, with the help of Hubert, a syndicate of artists led by the Reverend Jared Flagg (father of architect Ernest Flagg) began putting up the Rembrandt, a building of studios and apartments at 152 West 57 Street – demolished around 1970 and now the site of the Carnegie Hall Tower office building. Hubert Pirsson & Company were its architects, and the building application rendered the name of the owner as "Hubert Home Club." This was the concept of Phillip Hubert that would bring together wealthy men of "congenial" social status who would invest in a joint stock company that would erect an apartment house and then assign to each man a lease for a specific unit commensurate with the investment made. Additional units would be retained by the cooperative corporation that would be rented to outsiders, with the rental profits used to maintain the entire building for the benefit of the resident investors.

Apartments were traditionally investment ventures in which the developer would rent the individual residential units on a monthly or yearly basis to create a cash flow that would be sufficient to give him a return on his capital that he felt was sufficient to justify the time and effort it took to construct the building. The "Hubert Home Club" concept conflated the roles of owner and resident in much the same way a modern cooperative apartment house does. In a such a cooperative, the building is owned by the cooperative corporation, which is itself owned by its stockholders. Each stockholder holds the number of shares assigned to a particular apartment unit, with those shares entitling him to a proprietary lease on that apartment. A modern cooperative apartment house may include stores or doctors' offices that the cooperative can rent out to create an income stream to benefit the resident-owners. The Rembrandt substituted the income from tenant-occupied apartments, as the building had no stores or offices.

Following the success of the Rembrandt, in 1882 Flagg and Hubert erected a vastly larger Home Club cooperative apartment house at 121 Madison Avenue at the northeast corner of 29th Street. In place of the interlocking apartment arrangement of the Rembrandt that provided higher ceiling heights for the entertaining rooms and lower ceilings for the bedrooms and service spaces, the Madison Avenue structure accomplished the same result by providing only duplex units, with the entertaining rooms on one floor and the bedrooms on a floor directly above. The ceiling heights on the bedroom floor were lower than those on the floors that held the reception rooms (entrance hall, parlor, library, and dining room) Each pair of floors on Madison Avenue accommodated only five sprawling apartments. The building still exists, but stripped of its ornamentation, and totally rebuilt into small single-floor apartments lacking the grandeur and duplex arrangements of the original structure. The Hubert Home Club scheme was used again at an even larger scale in the construction of The Chelsea. Ultimately, that West 23rd Street venture failed as an upper-class apartment house, done in by a changing neighborhood, a changing economy, and the fickle nature

[ 7 ]

of many wealthy socially-mobile people. In 1905 it was converted to a hotel, going through several successive owners, and it continued until 2011 as a combination transient and residential hotel. In that year, transient guests were no longer accepted, and a major renovation was begun over, under, and around the remaining rent-regulated long-term residential tenants. Although The Chelsea began as one form of competition to the Dakota, it quickly lost that status to the larger, grander, and more financially stable uptown building.

The Osborne (the second of that name, erected nine years after the one on Fifth Avenue), which still exists at 205 West 57 Street (fig. 11), is a case study in the hazards to developers of the new upper-class luxury apartment house of the 1880s. The market for large luxury apartments was the same one for which the word home had always meant a single-family self-contained house. A small rowhouse, a grand brownstone, or even a huge limestone mansion, but always for one family only. To overcome the inherent prejudice against multi-family living, an exceptionally lavish product was planned. For developer Thomas Osborne this meant a massive Italian Renaissance palazzo of rusticated brownstone, with large, high-ceilinged apartments (fig. 64 on page 48), and enough bronze, marble, stained glass, mosaics, and exotic woods to impress even the most jaded of consumers. They may have impressed those who rented the apartments, but not the money-lenders.

FIG. 11. The Osborne, 205 West 57 Street, not yet finished, with a large white sign attached to the corner of the building where it could be read by passers-by, on which it is announced that the Fire Proof Apartment Building would be opening May 1st 1885. The sign can be read with a loupe on the original photograph. *courtesy of Brian Merlis*

Osborne over extended himself and was ultimately forced to declare bankruptcy and sell his building at a loss. Osborne had previously been a stone contractor, and after his building construction fiasco, he went back to supplying stone for others to use in their projects, avoiding speculative activities entirely. He had made the mistake of many investors before and since. He had borrowed large sums for the project without having sufficient reserve capital to carry the loans until rental income from the apartments would be sufficient to cover that expense. His over-confidence put the entire project at risk, and he lost the bet.

José de Navarro had a similar problem when he constructed the sprawling eight-building complex that became known as the Spanish Flats or the Navarro, at 59th Street and Seventh Avenue (fig. 12, and fig. 65 on page 49). Rather than building and holding the project as a rental venture, he had structured his finances so each building would become

FIG. 12. The Spanish Flats on West 59th Street, facing Central Park at Seventh Avenue. The photograph was taken about 1900 and published shortly after in a popular picture book of the city's buildings and activities. *King's Views of New York*

a cooperative corporation upon completion, thereby enabling him to take his money out as the buildings were finished and the apartments sold, presumably so that cash flow could finance the subsequent buildings. With that in mind, de Navarro and his architects Hubert Pirsson & Company planned the huge apartments very grandly and built them very lavishly. To keep down the selling price of each apartment, the buildings would be erected on leased land, although the cooperative corporation owning each building would have the right at any time to purchase the land under its building. The leased-land concept was to be the downfall of the entire venture. At the time construction costs began seriously exceeding the estimates and the available cash flow, ownership of the individual buildings had not yet been transferred to the individual cooperative corporations, so the mortgage holder J. Jennings McComb was able to foreclose on the entire project rather than on individual buildings alone. De Navarro lost his entire investment, and McComb completed the project as a complex of rental buildings. The original buyers of the co-op stock lost their investments.

Architect Philip Hubert had conceived of McComb's Spanish Flats project from the start as a complex of buildings that would be operated under a single central management, enabling him to solve a problem that had vexed him on smaller one-building ventures. Because the site spanned 58th to 59th streets along Seventh Avenue and extended 425 feet down the two streets, there was ample room for a private driveway that sloped down to the basement level

FIG. 13. The upper level of the interior courtyard of the Spanish Flats, mid-block between 58th and 59th Streets, with the fountains serving as skylights for the underground "street" for tradesmen and deliveries.

at the center of the block, allowing tradesmen to bring their delivery wagons and carts directly into an underground street that served the eight buildings. At the upper level, the residents looked down on floral fountains, which also served as skylights for the lower level (fig. 13). This off-street delivery concept, which was also used for the decorous removal of the garbage and ashes, was part of the planning at the Dakota as well.

The *Real Estate Record & Guide,* on 3 June 1882, commented somewhat breathlessly on the significant number of apartment houses being erected or projected to be built, saying "Before five years are over New York will have the largest and best appointed apartment houses in the world." (see Appendix E for the full text of the article).

Apartment rentals were not advertised in the 1880s the way they are today, but prices can be gleaned from a perusal of the *Real Estate Record & Guide* for the period. Here is a comparison of *annual* rentals for a few apartment houses that sought middle- and upper-income tenants.

| | | |
|---|---|---|
| The Spanish Flats | Seventh Avenue at 59th Street | $2000 to $7000 |
| The Dakota | Eighth Avenue at 72nd Street | $1500 to $5000 |
| The Berkshire | Madison Avenue at 52nd Street | $1500 to $4000 |
| The Dalhousie | 40 West 59 Street | $2000 to $2750 |
| The Gramercy | 34 Gramercy Park | $2000 to $4500 |
| The Palermo | 125 East 57 Street | $2500 |
| The Grenoble | 200 West 57 Street | $2500 |
| The Florence | 101 West 18 Street | $1600 to $2200 |

FIG. 14. The original Beresford apartment hotel on Central Park West from 81st to 82nd streets. The 1889 section is in the foreground, with the 1892 addition behind it. The dining room had been on the top floor of the first section; it was relocated to the top floor of the addition when that section was completed.

# CHAPTER 2

# Apartment Hotels: a hybrid form of residence

HISTORICALLY, hotels were rather disreputable places, often connected to a tavern or inn, where single travelling men could rent a bed or a room for the night. They served a useful purpose in the 18th and early 19th century, but "nice" people wouldn't choose to live in such places. The original John Jacob Astor made hotel living acceptable in 1836, the year he opened his large and luxurious Astor House on lower Broadway just to the north of St. Paul's Chapel. This impressively-grand block-long hostelry (and the others that followed it) catered to many of New York's upper-class visitors and wealthy residents. Until the first middle-class apartment house opened in 1870, these hotels were the only alternative to a one-family private house for socially well-placed New York families. Gradually, an alternative emerged – a completely residential or "family" hotel with few or no rooms for transients.

The original published reports about the Dakota when it was still an unbuilt project indicated that it would be a residential apartment hotel for families, although the building was actually developed as an apartment house, with spacious apartments. It also contained small flats and individual rooms, but they were available for rent solely by the guests of the residents, and its dining rooms were open to those residents and guests and not to the general public. That reality may have been a factor in the decision by millinery dealer Jacob Rothschild in 1889 to begin to assemble a block-long large piece of Central Park West property. The *Real Estate Record and Builders Guide* on 21 September 1889 reported on what was undoubtedly the first property acquired by Rothschild in accumulating the land for his projected (but unannounced and probably then unknown) Hotel Majestic.

### REAL ESTATE NEWS.
A quarter of a million dollars is the figure at which the choice plot of six lots on the southwest corner of Central Park West (8th avenue) and 72nd street is held.

Rothschild hired architect Alfred Zucker to design what opened in 1894 as the Hotel Majestic at the south corner of 72nd Street, across from the Dakota (figs. 15, 16 and 17). The new hotel offered the latest word in luxurious accommodations, and with a billiard room, bowling alleys, a ballroom, a ladies' writing room in the Egyptian style, and a roof garden, it served both well-heeled transient

FIG. 15. The Hotel Majestic across from the Dakota at Central Park West and 72nd Street in 1903. The building was not yet ten years old and was still a chic place for transient and semi-permanent visitors to stay. It freely rented its apartments and its private reception rooms to Jews at a time when many hotels did not, which doubtless helped its balance sheet. The proximity of the Park and good transportation facilities were a plus, as of course were the expansive views . *King's Views of New York*

FIG. 16. The Hotel Majestic about 1904, showing the Barnard apartment house (on the left in the picture) at the north end of the blockfront from 70th to 71st Streets where 101 Central Park West now stands. The Dakota appears on the right in the picture. *llustrated Post Card Co., New York and Germany*

visitors, and socially self-conscious families. Those families were the sort who either didn't want the bother of maintaining a complete brownstone row-house, or weren't willing to accept the "tenement living" of apartment houses, but weren't yet able to afford the grandeur of the Dakota.

As the Dakota and other apartment houses along Central Park West were developed, "family" hotels arose as alternatives. In addition to the Majestic, there was the San Remo, designed by Edward L. Angell and completed in two stages in 1891 between 74th and 75th Streets by Michael Brennan, a well-known building contractor, here acting as a real estate developer and operator (figure 148 on page 181). The Beresford was erected in two sections in 1889 and 1892 by Alva Walker on the blockfront from 81st to 82nd Streets, and featured non-housekeeping apartments, with meals taken by the residents in a dining room on the top floor overlooking Central Park. When the first section opened, the *Real Estate Record & Guide* provided a long description of the venture (see Appendix F for the full text of the article). The El Dorado, built in 1902 on the block between 90th and 91st Streets, was a pure apartment house with units as large as 14 rooms. Although its developer John Signell did not include restaurant facilities, he did provide a garage and battery charging room for the newly-popular electric automobiles. Its two-sectioned turreted design was the work of architects Neville & Bagge. The Majestic was the most southerly of those 19th century hostelries, and by far the most "majestic and well-patronized." The *Real Estate Record & Guide* on 28 September 1889 gave expanded coverage to the apartment hotel phenomenon and the new direction the increased West Side building activity was taking. (See Appendix G for the full text of the article). By the 1920s, fully housekeeping apartments with kitchens in each unit had become the standard for permanent family residences, with kitchen-less suites far less attractive and operation of the central dining and kitchen facilities unprofitable for the landlords. As transient hotels, the old family hotels were inefficient, ultimately resulting in their closure and the marketing of their large properties for comparably large but more modern ventures. The Majestic, the San Remo, the Beresford, and the El Dorado were all replaced between 1928 and 1932 by much larger apartment houses that preserve the names. All four new buildings were in the early planning stages long before the economy was wracked by the Great Depression, with the critical impetus for their development being the planning and construction of the new Independent Subway System along Central Park West.

FIG. 17. The entrance to the Hotel Majestic about 1920, showing at the left the 10-story Barnard apartments and the top mansard roof of the 12-story Lorington, both replaced by the current 101 Central Park West.

"THE DAKOTA"  NEW YORK CITY

SIMON FIELDHOUSE

FIG. 18. A pen-and-ink-plus-watercolor drawing of the Dakota by Simon Fieldhouse of Sydney, Australia

# CHAPTER 3

# The Builder of the Dakota: Edward Clark

EDWARD CLARK was an exceptional man. He was an astute evaluator of people and ideas and a man able to balance the conflicting aspects of his life in ways that allowed him to succeed where others saw only impassible obstacles. He saw big pictures that lesser men couldn't even imagine, and then made them happen by relentless hard work and minute attention to details. Again and again he accomplished outstanding results. In many ways he was a 19th century Steve Jobs – a man who used his imagination to create markets that few had even dreamed existed using his brilliance to create new products that met unarticulated needs and applying his pervasive penchant for hard work to amass a huge fortune. And at the end of his life, he created a grand product that opened the door to an essential element of New York City's growth and prosperity: the luxury apartment house.

To all outward appearances, Edward Clark was a sober, quiet, gracious, generous, ever-proper, classically educated, religiously conservative, modest, and utterly conventional lawyer (fig. 19). He was born on 19 December 1811 in the tiny town of Athens in Greene County, New York to an establishment upper-middle class family. His father Nathan Clark owned a successful pottery works, and his mother Julia Nichols Clark brought up Edward in a religious household where prudence, modesty, and generosity were the qualities to be both admired and enacted. Nathan Clark's business acuity in expanding his company and monopolizing his market doubtless was observed by his son, along with his love of learning. Edward had ample time to absorb their influence; his father reached the age of 92 and his mother 90.

Following an initial education under a private tutor at home, and then Latin lessons at a local school, he spent four years at a boarding academy in Lenox, Massachusetts, where he was said to have read every one of the 500 or so books in the school's library. From there he enrolled in

FIG. 19. Edward Clark as a young man

Williams College, from which he graduated in 1831. Following the apprentice-method of legal education of the time, that year Clark started work at the law office of Ambrose L. Jordan in Hudson, New York. Learning enough from his mentor to be admitted to the bar, he established a legal practice in Poughkeepsie, New York from 1833 to 1837 when he entered into the partnership of Jordan & Clark. Shortly thereafter the firm moved their offices to New York City where they remained law partners until 1863. Clark had already become his partner's son-in-law when he married Caroline Jordan in 1835 and she gave birth to their first son the following year.

In 1848, a client sought legal help from Jordan & Clark, a client who would have a greater impact on New York and indeed on the entire world than he could have ever imagined. But a client so distasteful in appearance and demeanor that Ambrose Jordan would have nothing to do with him and instead asked his junior partner to take care of the man's problems on his own. This 6-foot-4-inch bear of a man was Isaac Merritt Singer, who in every respect would appear to be at the other end of the spectrum from Edward Clark.

Although born in 1811 in upstate New York, just as Clark was, his background was completely different. Instead of material comforts and a good education, Singer grew up in abject poverty, leaving home at age twelve to work as an unskilled laborer wherever he could find a job, until at age nineteen he started working in a machine shop, where he discovered his strong mechanical aptitude and inventive creativity. Singer, with his first wife and child, lived an itinerant life for nine years, during which he developed (alongside his tinkering skills) his skill at acting, working in theater companies and tool shops, and getting involved in various schemes. As a result of one such initiative with one of his brothers, he invented a machine for drilling in rock and in 1839 obtained a patent for it. Later he invented a device that could carve wood-block type. It was this second invention that had title problems and for which he sought assistance from Clark. After resolving the problems, Clark helped Singer obtain patent protection for the carving device, which was granted in 1849. When in 1850 he was still unable to pay Clark his fee, the lawyer instead accepted a three-eighths ownership interest in the patent. With that agreement, a business marriage of two opposites was set in place.

Fig. 20. Isaac Merritt Singer in 1869, age 58

Where Clark was refined, self-effacing, hard-working, and religious; Singer was uncouth, a self-promoter, indolent, and completely amoral (ultimately he fathered 24 children by five women) (fig. 20). But by nature both men thought outside the box and could imagine what might be, without feeling a need to know beforehand whether the concept was feasible or even possible. Both men acknowledged that their personal styles and lives were essentially incompatible, but that the ways in which their minds worked were surprisingly similar. They saw the mutual benefits of working together and proceeded to do exactly that.

Sewing machines of one sort or another had existed since an English patent was issued for one in 1790, yet it wasn't until 1846 that Elias Howe Jr. was issued a patent for a practical one. But even Howe's machine had problems. Sniffing a potential pot of gold, Singer worked on each of the problems in turn, and in short order came up with a distinctive new machine that worked better than any before. He found financial backers, created a company to build a prototype, and then in 1851 received a patent. The only trouble was that one critical aspect of it was identical to one of the claims of the patent of Elias Howe, who quickly brought an infringement lawsuit. Again Singer went to Clark to find a way through the problem.

Isaac Singer still had no money to pay for the legal help he desperately needed, but he had a product he believed in and a company to make it. Although Clark clearly perceived and disliked the flamboyance and brutish ways of the hard-living inventor who seemed ready to crash and burn at every turn, he was, beneath his conservative exterior, a risk taker. He was willing to back someone whose lack of cash and couth was counterbalanced by an unusually fertile and inventive mind. He proposed that he would defend Singer's sewing machine in return for one-third ownership of the company that would manufacture it. Singer accepted the offer. Clark then bought out the other small investors who had gotten the venture started, leaving him and Singer as equal owners of what would shortly become I.M. Singer & Company. He also extracted from the inventor a 50-percent ownership interest in all of Singer's future patents, plus the right to control the company's management. In one fell swoop he established the financial and structural foundation for a machine that would change the lives of millions of people around the world. And he opened the chute through which the money would flow to create a fortune and establish the Clark family dynasty.

As half-owner of the Singer company, Clark proved a brilliant businessman who made canny decisions, one after another. He was overseer of every aspect of how the company made money, expanding the scope of its operations, moving it from upstate to New York City and then opening branches of the renamed Singer Manufacturing Company. He hired sales agents who combined technical knowledge and skills with an ability to promote the machine effectively. He changed the way the machines looked, advertised them creatively, gave selective discounts to women such as ministers' wives whose opinions and activities would likely generate more sales. He accepted old machines as trade-ins for new ones, and he created an installment plan under which a machine could be paid for over time.

Then in 1856 he created the "Sewing Machine Combination" as a patent pool in which large manufacturing concerns formed an alliance that ended the battles among countless competing small sewing machine companies. By controlling all the relevant patents (at least until 1877 when the last of them expired) he insured the domination of Singer. Of course if this were today, this Combination would have been sunk immediately as a monopoly, or restraint of trade, but such consumer protections were nonexistent in the 19th century. A bigger obstacle to a total monopoly was that patent expiration problem, which would open the field to cheap imitations. In another bold maneuver, Clark cut the price of a particularly popular machine by 50 percent. At $30 for cash or $40 if paid over time, the machine was a bargain hard to resist. Even before his new competitors could gear up following the end of the critical patent protection, Clark had created a natural monopoly based on price and guaranteed by volume. It would be virtually impossible for any newcomer to match that price on a machine that would be anywhere near as good.

To ensure the company's long term stability, Clark invested some of the profits in rock-solid safe securities. Even though their yield was low, those investments provided stability during slack periods, acting as a cushion to absorb the financial volatility of uneven sales in hard times. In a similar fashion, Clark's policy of owning the company's real estate instead of renting it insured its prosperity would be secure even in a bad economy.

Edward Clark had foresight lacking in ordinary people. He took the task of sewing, which had been a staple of living for thousands of years, and created a *desire* to sew among a class of women who would never have dreamed of doing so, of sitting in front of a complicated machine and operating it. He didn't invent the Singer sewing machine, he invented and perfected the means and methods for building it, advertising it, marketing it, selling it, and making money from it. He started out as a lawyer and used his understanding of how the law worked to harness it to build a business. And from that business he built a fortune.

Fig. 21. Edward Clark, about age 60

In 1877 Edward Clark was 66 years old (fig. 21). Judging from his business accomplishments, he clearly was in his prime. His father was still alive at age 89 as well as his mother. He doubtless anticipated living a long time, but perhaps anticipated as well that diversifying a significant portion of his assets into income-producing real estate would provide a reliable source of funds for his grandchildren and their children. To that end he had ideas that must have been percolating through his mind for more than a few years.

Clark had traveled abroad a great deal to expand the Singer business and as an unusually observant man, he would have seen how the urban centers of Paris, London, Edinburgh, and other great European cities had always had rowhouses just as New York, but they also had apartment houses. French ideas about housing middle-class families had already taken root in New York after the Stuyvesant apartments on East 18th Street had opened. New York's growth since the Civil War had generated a significant need for housing at all levels, and Clark clearly concluded not only that he could make money from money by investing in New York City real estate, but how to do it.

It is not known whether Edward Clark had worked out any master plan for what he ultimately wanted to build, and where he wanted to build it, but he started out with a bang in 1877 by acquiring in fairly quick succession four major pieces of Manhattan. In north-to-south order, they were:

    a. The block between Eighth and Ninth Avenues from 86th to 85th Streets
    b. The block between Eighth and Ninth Avenues from 74th to 73rd Streets
    c. The block between Eighth and Ninth Avenues from 73rd to 72nd Streets
    d. The block between Broadway and Seventh Avenue from 56th to 55th Streets
    e. Two lots on the southeast and southwest corners of Seventh Avenue and 55th Streets

Plots a. and c. fronted on major extra-wide streets offering direct access to Central Park, and plots d. and e. were not far from the southern end of the Park and its entrance at Seventh Avenue.

These locations were obviously not selected randomly, and that all four originally appeared to have approximately comparable value suggests that he perhaps had in mind leaving them to his four grandsons. In fact, each of those young men did inherit one of those plots, even though the eldest was only 12 when his grandfather died and the youngest was but a few months old.

While we don't know what specific plans Clark entertained for his properties beyond what he actually built, some insight into his thought process can be gained by considering a paper he delivered in 1879 at a meeting of the West End Association, a group of wealthy men who had bought property on the Upper West Side or who were interested in its development. Clark's speech that evening revealed a vision for the development of the Upper West Side that was far-reaching and amazingly prescient. In many ways Clark presented an approach to city planning that would seem valid even today. He advocated large-scale construction of apartment houses for the middle classes, and he outlined a justification for the grandly luxurious housing projects he soon proceeded to build himself. But he also saw a need for decent apartment houses for the working classes, where there would be adequate space and facilities provided for each family, with steam heat, good air, and light, in fireproof buildings with elevators. Moreover, he foresaw the need to plan such housing on the scale of full-blocks, rather than the 25-foot-wide lots then standard for tenements. He even proposed methods for financing the construction of these projects. (see Appendix A for the full text of Clark's paper) These pioneering efforts at urban planning and development were only partially undertaken before Clark's untimely death three years later truncated whatever grand scheme he may have harbored. A land map published in 1885 encompassing West 72nd Street to West 74th Street shows the Dakota at Central Park West, the two small apartment buildings at the northern corners of 73rd Street and Columbus Avenue, and the two long rows of single-family houses along the north side of 73rd Street, all of which Clark had built (fig. 22). The unadorned plain-brick western wall of the Dakota strongly suggests that Clark likely intended to construct a second apartment house of comparable size immediately to the west of it, and his ownership of the entire remainder of the block pointed to its completion with some mix of apartment buildings and row houses, probably with shops beneath the elevated railway along Columbus Avenue.

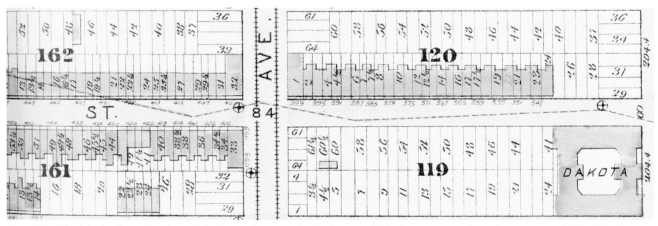

FIG. 22. The blocks from 72nd to 74th Street showing the Dakota and Clark's two sets of row houses as published in the 1885 edition of the Robinson Atlas of New York City.

Edward Clark had bought property at three of the four corners at the intersection of Seventh Avenue and 55th Street (fig. 23). On the fourth corner was the building of Tattersalls (of New York) Limited, containing a circular arena in which horse auctions were held to serve the many stables in the neighborhood (fig. 24).

FIG. 23. The intersection of Seventh Avenue and 55th Street, showing the Van Corlear, the Ontiora, and the Wyoming apartment houses built by Clark, with Tattersalls circular horse auction building on the remaining corner.
*Robinson Atlas of New York City 1885*

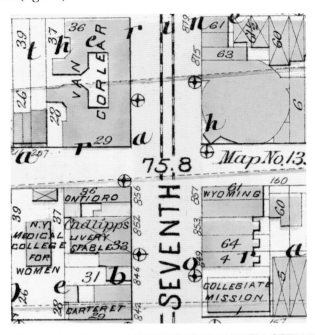

FIG. 24. The building of Tattersalls (of New York) Limited, containing a circular arena in which horse auctions were held to serve the many stables in the neighborhood.

Below is a chronology, strongly suggesting that Clark had deliberately laid out for himself a general plan of how he intended to create a West Side real estate empire.

1877    Clark makes major purchases of unimproved real estate.

1878    Clark has architect Henry Janeway Hardenbergh begin the Van Corlear apartment house on the west side of Seventh Avenue from 55th to 56th Streets.

1879    Clark has Hardenbergh begin a small apartment house and 24 rowhouses on the north side of 73rd Street west from Columbus Avenue towards Amsterdam Avenue (Hardenbergh's father moves into one of them at 121 West 73 Street).

1880    Clark has Hardenbergh begin the Wyoming apartment house at the southeast corner of Seventh Avenue and 55h Street.

1880    Clark has Hardenbergh begin the Dakota.

1882    Clark has Hardenbergh begin a small apartment house and 27 rowhouses on the north side of 73rd Street east from Columbus Avenue towards Central Park West.

1882    Clark has Hardenbergh begin the Ontiora apartment house at the southwest corner of Seventh Avenue and 55th Street

1882    Clark dies on October 14th.

The 17 October 1882 edition of the *New York Tribune* published this obituary of Edward Clark:

Edward Clark, one of the founders of the Singer Manufacturing Company and its president for several years, died at his country residence in Cooperstown, N.Y. on Saturday, from typhoid malaria. He was born in Athens, Greene County, on December 19, 1811. His father, Nathan Clark, long carried on a successful manufacturing business at that place, dying about two years ago at the age of ninety-two. His mother was the daughter of John Nichols of Waterbury, Conn. Edward Clark was educated at Williams College, being graduated in 1830. In the same year he began the study of law in the office of Ambrose L. Jordan, at Hudson, N.Y. In 1833 Mr. Clark began to practice at Poughkeepsie, but four years later he formed a law partnership with Mr. Jordan and the firm removed to this city, where they carried on a very successful business. Later, William L. Dayton, of New Jersey, who ran as vice-president on the Freemont Presidential ticket, became a member of the firm. it was while in the law business that Mr. Clark first became interested in the manufacture of Singer sewing machines. Isaac M. Singer, the inventor, in 1848, was a client of Mr. Clark's firm, but his means were not sufficient to enable him to carry on the litigation with Elias Howe, Jr., and others, who claimed that Mr. Singer was infringing their patents. The promising future of these inventions was apparent to Mr. Clark, who assisted with his means and legal skill the needy inventor in conducting the litigation and developing the business of sewing machine manufacture. The firm of I. M. Singer & Co. was formed in 1848, and as their success became more assured Mr. Clark gradually abandoned his law practice, doing little in that line after 1851. Owing to a want of entire harmony in the policy of the firm, both partners, in 1865, retired from the active management of the business, which was transferred to the stock company organized under the name it now bears. Both Mr. Singer and Mr. Clark were directors in the company, and Mr. Singer dying in 1875, in the following year Mr. Clark was elected president, retaining that position until his death.

In 1851 Mr. Clark purchased the property in Cooperstown which was formerly the home of the late John A. Dix. There he built a country residence named Fernleigh, where he generally lived about four months of the year. He early took an interest in the Central Railroad of New-Jersey, and to his holdings of the company's stock in the days of its prosperity he continually added purchases made through the period of its bankruptcy. He was one of the active supporters of Garrett-Gowen combination, which secured the control of the company in the last election, when he was chosen a director. When he died Mr. Clark was one of the largest stockholders in the corporation. He also made considerable and profitable investments in bonds and stocks of other corporations. He held nearly one half of the stock of the Singer Manufacturing Company.

About seven years ago Mr. Clark invested heavily in real estate on the west side of this city, which he immediately improved. In 1878 he built the Vancorlear apartment house at Seventh ave. and Fifty-sixth-st. Subsequently he built the Wyoming opposite the Vancorlear, and about the same time he paid $250,000 for the land on which the Dakota apartment house in West Seventy-second and Seventy-third sts. is now building. Mr. Clark was probably the largest owner of real estate on the west side near Central Park. He also owned much real estate in the West and in the counties in New-Jersey adjacent to New-York City. His wealth is estimated at between $15,000,000 and $20,000,000. He was an active member of the West Side Association.

Mr. Clark's private charities were numerous. His generosity contributed largely to the improvement of Cooperstown, and Williams College was a recipient of his bounty. Besides large sums of money which he contributed to that institution, he erected a handsome building on the college grounds for museum purposes, which has been named Clark Hall. He also recently was the principal contributor to the building of the Episcopalian Church of Centerville, Passaic County, N.J. Mr. Clark was a genial man, not extravagant and undemonstrative. He married Miss Jordan, a daughter of his former law partner. His wife died several years ago, and his only child that he leaves is his son Alfred C. Clark. The funeral will take place today at Cooperstown.

FIG. 25. The Dakota as drawn by W.P. Snyder for Harper's Weekly, February 27, 1886.

# CHAPTER 4

# The Architect of the Dakota: Henry Janeway Hardenbergh

B EST KNOWN for the Dakota and the Plaza Hotel, erected in 1907 at Fifth Avenue and Central Park South, Henry Janeway Hardenbergh (figs. 26 and 27) left an indelible legacy to New York City. Born in New Brunswick, New Jersey on 6 February 1847, to an old Dutch family that had arrived in the New World from Holland in 1644, he was the great-great-grandson of the Rev. Jacob Rutsen Hardenbergh the founder of Rutgers College, and the son of John Pool Hardenbergh, an importer.

The young Hardenbergh apprenticed to the German-born architect Detlef Lienau in 1863 and struck out on his own around 1870. Among his early commissions for Edward Clark was the 1876 Kingfisher Tower, a 60-foot-high folly on a lake at Cooperstown, New York, that was a sham castle based loosely on 12th and 13th century French châteaux (fig. 42 on page 31). In New York City, his earliest design was the 1878 Van Corlear apartment house on the west side of Seventh Avenue, from 55th to 56th Street (figs. 28 and 29). A mix of Dutch and Queen Anne styling, the Van Corlear – demolished in 1922 – was described by the *Real Estate Record & Guide* in 1878 as "the most extensive apartment house in New York, in which almost all the apartments were taken before completion, no doubt pleasing its developer, Edward Clark." Built for 36 families at a cost of about $10,000 per unit, the Van Corlear was classed as a French flat – for it was to France that America still looked for instruction in the art and techniques of developing communal dwelling spaces. At about 2,000 square feet per apartment, each was on the scale of a private house (fig. 61 on page 46). The Van Corlear made a significant splash, for it was the largest and most thoughtfully planned apartment house constructed up to that time and appears to be an amalgamation of the ideas of both Clark and Hardenbergh, just as the Singer Sewing Machine enterprise amalgamated the complementary ideas and strengths of Clark and Singer. Three very long and detailed articles about the new building project were published in April 1878. (See Appendices B, C, and D for their complete texts).

Hardenbergh connected with Clark at an auspicious time, just as Clark was beginning a building campaign that included property purchased on West 72nd and 73rd Streets. In 1879 they began 25 row houses at 103-151 West 73 Street (fig. 30), a simple Victorian row. Only the house at 103 survives, along with the small apartment house Hardenbergh designed at the northwest corner of

Fig. 26. Henry Hardenbergh as a mature architect.

Fig. 27. Henry Hardenbergh as a young man.

Columbus and 73rd built at the same time. The rowhouses were also built for about $10,000 apiece, several cuts above the typical price for a brownstone.

Next came the Dakota. Hardenbergh's German Renaissance motifs flowered here, along with Edward Clark's ambitious goal for a comfortable upper-class apartment building. A glowing review of the Dakota by the *Real Estate Record & Guide* in 1884 ended with the observation that "the owners have been fortunate in their architect, and Mr. Hardenbergh has been fortunate in his clients."

This good fortune continued when Clark proceeded to build another, better-known row of picturesque houses at 13-63 West 73 Street, just opposite the Dakota (fig. 31). These were built for an impressive $15,000 apiece as a varied row of buff and red brick, with sober but intelligent detailing in Nova Scotia stone, the most sophisticated large group of rowhouses to be built at that time. When Clark built the picturesque little Ontiora apartment house, at 55th Street and Seventh Avenue (fig. 32) and the similarly-sized original Wyoming apartment house across the avenue, Hardenbergh got both commissions. The Ontiora survives, as do many of the houses.

After Clark died in 1882, his family ended its association with Hardenbergh, but the architect's reputation was established. His work was "thoughtful, thorough and scholarly," the *Record & Guide* said; he designed buildings for long-term use, not short-term profit, and his insistence on heavy, conservative masonry designs increased his reputation for dependable solidity.

This suited estates and companies well, so it was natural that the Astors hired him for their Bavarian-style nine-story building at 10 Wall Street (demolished around 1930). And the Western Union Telegraph Company retained him for several buildings, including the picturesque little structure that still survives at the southwest corner of 23rd Street and Fifth Avenue (fig. 33), described by the *Architectural Record* as "one of the happiest bits of our street architecture."

He also worked for the Rhinelander estate, designing a handful of informal red-brick row houses, among them 337-339 East 87 Street (1887). Like Clark, the Schermerhorns also built for the long term, and in 1887 Hardenbergh designed the six-story building at the northwest corner of Lafayette and Great Jones for William C. Schermerhorn, restored and given a new life in 2000. The dwarf columns on the ground floor, eccentric end bays (which hold the elevators and stairways) and richly modeled terra cotta and stone work combine to make a wonderfully chunky masterpiece, especially for an industrial building (fig. 34).

A review in the *Real Estate Record & Guide* in 1889 called the Schermerhorn Building "a cred-

FIG. 28. The Van Corlear, on Seventh Avenue between 55th and 56th Streets, with the Ontiora under construction at the left on the southwest corner of 55th Street. *Royal Institute of British Architects RIBA 13673*

FIG. 29. The avenue frontage of The Van Corlear in 1915, showing the dry moat protected by an ornamental iron railing, a feature that was repeated in the Dakota. On the far side of 56th Street is the Grenoble Hotel. On the opposite side of Seventh Avenue is the plain white brick side wall of the Alwyn Court apartment house, and beyond it, the twin turrets of the Central Park Apartments or Spanish Flats. *New York City Transit Museum Archives (722) R4&3654 STR 116+40*

FIG. 30. The row houses and two small apartment houses on the north side of West 73rd Street on both sides of the elevated railway that ran along Columbus Avenue

FIG. 31. The 1882 small apartment house at the corner of 9th Avenue, with the adjoining rowhouses along 73rd Street, from the Dakota roof, with the elevated railway tracks and the Hudson River beyond. *New-York Historical Society, negative #72163*

itable work, tried by the strictest standards. As things go, it is very good indeed." In 1966 it became the first of Hardenbergh's buildings to be designated a New York City landmark, the Dakota's designation coming three years later.

In the 1890s, the Astors returned to Hardenbergh for the stupendously picturesque Waldorf-Astoria Hotel, built in two sections on Fifth Avenue from 33rd to 34th Streets and later replaced by the Empire State Building. There, the architect hewed more closely to the Germanic Renaissance, putting giant spires, balconies, porches and dormers on this red-brick and brownstone hostelry, among the most famous in the city's history (fig. 35).

The 13-story Wolfe Building, built in 1895 at William Street and Maiden Lane but demolished in 1974 and forgotten now, was widely praised as a solution to the problem of skyscraper design (fig. 36). This Flemish-style building was capped with huge stepped gables – some as big as a row house – and a clock. The building with its varied angles cascaded down to the street in brilliantly contrasting red and buff brick.

FIG. 32. The Ontiora at the southwest corner of 55th Street and Seventh Avenue. The photograph was taken in 1922 during the demolition of the Van Corlear, which shows in the lower right-hand corner. The Ontiora originally had a single apartment of about 2000 square feet on each floor, fitted out in similar fashion as the Dakota, which was still under construction at the time this much smaller version was begun. Later subdivided to produce three units per floor, the building survives and has been refurbished with an apparent gradual conversion to commercial usage. *Irving Underhill, Museum of the City of New York*

FIG. 33. The Western Union Telegraph Building in 1884 at the southwest corner of Fifth Avenue and 23rd Street is seven stories of red brick with the top floor under a sloping roof with dormer windows. Its elaborate terra cotta plaque announcing the name of its original owner/occupant is still in view at the side-street entrance. *Royal Institute of British Architects RIBA 13672*

FIG. 34. The Schermerhorn Building on Lafayette Street
*Kenneth Grant*

Then, in the new century, Hardenbergh got four plum hotel commissions: the Willard in Washington (1902), the Plaza (1907) (fig. 37), the Martinique at 32nd Street and Broadway (1910) (figs. 38 and 39), and Boston's Copley-Plaza (1912). These firmly established him as a specialist in steel-frame hotel design. But he was also proud of his smaller buildings, like the Art Students' League at 215 West 57 Street, designed in 1891 (fig. 41), and the All Angels' Church Parish House, at 251 West 80 Street, designed in 1904 (after the nearby All Angels' Church was demolished for a modern apartment house, the congregation united its worship with its other activities in the Parish House). He also did a relatively small but ultra-luxurious apartment house at 787 Fifth Avenue for the Van Norden Trust Company, which occupied the ground floor (fig. 40).

Hardenbergh was still at work when World War I limited new construction and interrupted his career, he died in 1918 before the economy recovered and he could resume. Personal information on Henry Hardenbergh is scarce. He alternated living in New York and New Jersey, first at the Clark-owned rowhouse at 121 West 73 Street, then in Jersey City and Bernardsville, and later in a big town house of his own design at 12 East 56 Street. The 1900 census describes him as widowed, but he apparently had no children. For a time he practiced with John P. Hardenbergh Jr. and Adriance Hardenbergh, apparently his brother and nephew, respectively. He was a member of the Century Association, the Grolier Club and other clubs. At his death he was living in an apartment at 40 East 62 Street, an unusual neo-Medieval multi-dwelling designed by Albert Joseph Bodker with an exceptionally colorful and animated façade that made extensive use of terra-cotta ornament, indeed precisely the kind of apartment that an architect of Hardenbergh's taste and skill would find attractive, and oddly relate to the folly of 1875 that he designed for Edward Clark near Cooperstown, New York (fig. 42).

Hardenbergh maintained a proprietary interest in his buildings long after he had parted company with the client. Responding to an article about the Dakota in which the critic complained that delivery wagons were using the Dakota's main street-level courtyard, he wrote a letter, which the *American Architect and Building News* published on January 20, 1891 (page 31).

FIG. 35. Waldorf-Astoria Hotel. Hardenbergh's hotels were grandly ornate and skillfully planned for expansion. His Waldorf-Astoria was a major new hotel on a much larger adjoining lot serving as a major expansion of his earlier Waldorf Hotel. While he was careful to make them visually and functionally compatible in plan and floor alignments, it was really a case of the tail wagging the dog. Both the Plaza Hotel and the Hotel Martinique were designed for the later expansions effected when adjacent properties were acquired.
Byron, *King's Views of New York*

FIG. 36. John Wolfe Build-ing *King's Views of New York*

FIG. 37. The Plaza Hotel, c.1907
*King's Views of New York*

FIG. 38. Hotel Martinique
*King's Views of New York*

FIG. 39. Marquee of the Hotel Martinique

FIG. 40. 787 Fifth Avenue, c. 1908, on the southeast corner of 60th Street was a luxury apartment house with a single grand apartment on each floor, above a banking office for the Van Norden Trust Company. *King's Views of New York*

FIG. 41. The Art Students' League on the right at 221 West 57 Street, built originally for the American Fine Arts Society, with the Art Students' League as a tenant, along with the Architectural League and the American Artists. It adjoined a private equestrian club and riding ring built by George J. Gould for himself and some of his friends. To its east was a small old frame dwelling which later was taken down to provide space for an expansion of the Osborne apartment house at the corner of 57th Street and Seventh Avenue. At the left in the picture is an early apartment house. *King's View of New York*

## TO THE EDITORS OF THE AMERICAN ARCHITECT:—

Dear Sir, – I regret being called on so soon again to ask for space in your journal for a correction, but a statement in the article on "Apartment-Houses" in your issue of January, 17, seems to make it necessary.

The author, in referring to the "Dakota," says: "The only criticism to be made upon it, but a serious one, is that the service entrances to the suites are situated upon the same court-yard, so that grocers wagons and ice-carts are almost always to be seen standing about in the space which should lie reserved exclusively for more fashionable equipages, and for the promenades of the tenants of the house."

The fact is, that a grocer's wagon has never been seen within the quiet precincts of this court-yard, and an ice-cart would cause as much consternation to the aristocratic tenants as a street-car trundled into the space.

The error, on the part of your author, very probably and naturally arose from not having at hand a basement plan of the building — which I believe has never been published.

Underneath the court, the pavement of which is carried on arches, is a sub-court of precisely the same dimensions, lighted by two large openings, shown on plan. This is reached by a driveway at the rear on Seventy-third Street, of easy incline from the street-level, and a passageway under the building on the westerly side. In this sub-court are received all the commodities of housekeeping and all supplies for the tenants or house proper. The household goods of arriving or departing tenants are here received or discharged, and all garbage or ashes here removed. The service elevators and staircases start from this level, and servants are obliged to enter or leave the house through this court alone.

The arrangement has proved very successful and has attained precisely what your author lamented as lacking, namely, perfect quiet and seclusion for the main court-yard.

Very truly yours,

H. J. HARDENBERGH

FIG. 42. Kingfisher Tower, off the eastern shore of Otsego Lake near Cooperstown, New York. A folly designed by Henry Hardenbergh and built circa 1876 by Edward Clark to enhance the view.

FIG. 43. A romanticized drawing of the Dakota as published in the 7 September 1889 issue of Frank Leslie's Newspaper. Its caption read: "The contrast between the buildings erected in New York in recent years—massive, costly, and rich in decoration—and the humble little cottages which formerly occupied their sites is indeed most striking. Such a contrast can be found near Central Park in many places. Our artist has availed himself of the opportunity to make a picture that well illustrates the subject. The great overshadowing mass of brick and stone rises as if it would overwhelm the humble cottage that was built upon the plot when it was all a part of a garden or a farm. We see in the one wealth, luxury, and refinement, in the other the humble home of the poor. Who shall say that there is more happiness on the former than the latter?"

# CHAPTER 5

# The Upper West Side

T HE GEOGRAPHY and geology of Manhattan Island have had a strong impact on how the city developed, yet of equal importance has been the long line of business decisions of many individuals and organizations over many decades, with earlier ones affecting later ones. The direction, timing, and pace of real estate development in Manhattan resulted from the interplay between the ever-shifting ambitions of the men (and occasionally women) who sought to turn capital into cash flow, and the fixed reality of the ground beneath their feet and the water surrounding that ground.

Initially, there wasn't any East or West side, as all of New York comprised the lower end of Manhattan, which was too small to be considered anything but a single settlement. Nonetheless, even in the beginning, development tended to favor the East River side over the side fronting on the Hudson or North River; its currents and gentler flow were more favorable to ships, and thus to commerce. That easterly bias resulted in the creation of fill-land that extended the commercially-buildable ground-area out into the river. Water Street was where the land originally met the river. In the 18th century, the front edge of that boundary shifted to Front Street, as cribbing filled with unwanted materials became land on which new structures could be built. Once the economy of the newly-created country rebounded following the end of the hostilities with England, the process of creating new land resumed, extending the shoreline of Manhattan out to South Street.

As commerce extended north along the East River, so too did the creation of country estates on the high ground back from the river's edge where the air was fresher and the views better. Serving those estates, and connecting to Connecticut and eventually to Boston, were the north-running Boston Post Road and Eastern Post Road. Ferries at several points connected Manhattan to Long Island, generating cross roads and further development. Even the remote village of Harlem far to the north was expanding and generating investments by speculators. The real estate pot was beginning to simmer.

In 1831, Thomas Addis Emmet and others who owned land up in Harlem obtained a charter for the New York and Harlem Railroad. If they could connect the northern village with the larger southern settlements, their properties would increase significantly in value. Late in 1832 they began to do just that, with the opening of the first link. It consisted of horsecars on iron rails from the original station at Prince Street up to 14th Street. The *Morning Courier and Enquirer* forecast a new age of suburban living about to dawn in the distant outposts of 59th, 86th, and even 125th

FIG. 44. Rock removal at 81 Street and 9th Avenue in 1886 Robert Bracklow, Museum of the City of New York 207065

FIG. 45. Brennan house at 84th Street and Broadway in 1879 *New-York Historical Society negative #84696d*

FIG. 46. Southeast from the American Museum of Natural History in 1877, the year that Edward Clark bought the Dakota block and the one north of it. There is nothing on the Dakota site in this photo, and only small frame buildings on the other block.
*G.L. Feuardent courtesy of the American Museum of Natural History negative #337160*

street: "Instead of being cramped and confined to a single lot of ground and a close atmosphere in the city, an acre or two will be purchased and a home built at reduced expense, a garden, orchard, dairy and other conveniences to follow." Service to Murray Hill began in 1833, and in 1834 the trains went all the way up to Yorkville on surface-level tracks that ran along Fourth Avenue.

Relatively rapid transportation is an important incentive to real estate development, and the initial decisions of the 1831 incorporators established the foundation for that system. In 1853 the options were expanded when a horsecar line was opened on Third Avenue running at first from the lower East Side to the mid-Sixties. The line was replaced in 1878 by the elevated trains of the Third Avenue Railway. Cornelius Vanderbilt expanded on that East Side bias by building the first Grand Central Depot in 1871, and then lowering the train tracks along Fourth Avenue between then and 1875. During the four decades from the original 1831 charter to the opening of the train depot in 1871, builders of all stripes were creating spotty real estate developments throughout the East Side, and gradually filling in the vacant spaces. By the beginning of the 1880s, Manhattan east of Central Park had been built up with buildings and businesses, was attracting people, and producing profits.

But what of the West Side? Why wasn't it included in this expanding development? It too had a horsecar line that clip-clopped its way up Eighth Avenue, and it too experienced the 1879 opening all the way to 155th Street of the Ninth Avenue elevated railway. But from 1830 to 1870 it missed the steady northward traffic enjoyed by the other side of town because it lacked the East River attractions generating it. And its rocky geology and elevated topography discouraged construction. Everywhere, boulders blocked builders (fig. 44). Where streets had been cut through, pre-existing houses were often left isolated high above the roadway (fig. 45).

The farmhouse of Patrick and Mary Brennan at 84th Street near Broadway was where Edgar Allan Poe lived for a time. Antedating the street grid of 1811, it was accessible only by a long wooden stairway after the street was laid out and graded.

Part of the problem with the West Side was that the underlying rock (Manhattan schist in most of the area) varied considerably in elevation. Within the space of only a few blocks, it could be high above the grade established for the local streets, or far below that grade. In one respect this was an advantage, as it allowed the spoil taken from the high areas to build up the low (figs. 46,

FIG. 47. Southwest from the American Museum of Natural History in 1877 *G.L. Feuardent courtesy of the American Museum of Natural History negative #39367*

FIG. 48. South from the Elevated Railway station at 81st Street and Columbus Avenue in 1889. In the left-center is the first building of the American Museum of Natural History. In the haze beyond is the north façade of the Dakota. *New-York Historical Society negative #40835*

47, and 48). This process of leveling and filling was a direct outgrowth of the rectilinear grid that the three planning commissioners imposed on the entire island following their appointment in 1807. This right-angled layout of avenues and streets that virtually ignored the existing topography made almost no allowances for the sometimes-dramatic changes in elevation of the original land mass. Manhattan's foundation of rock was formed by prehistoric land upheavals and the relentless grinding of glacial advance and retreat (fig. 49). The commissioners' decision to maintain the straightness of the roadways and not to bend them around any topographical obstacles created elevation changes so great that they forced roadways to uncomfortable angles upward and downward, as at Lexington Avenue and 102nd Street, or in the 140s between Broadway and Riverside Drive. It was only when the original planning was extended north of 155th Street that the roadway construction made concessions to the reality of the ancient geology and its considerable differences in surface elevation.

Back down in the West 70s those topographic extremes were more manageable than at the northern end of the island, but they nonetheless imposed hardships on builders. The city might level the streets, but it was the land owners who were responsible for bringing their properties up (or down) to street level. The expense of doing this acted as a severe restriction on real estate development. When combined with the lack of public transportation, developers generally looked elsewhere. But all wasn't totally vacant, and by 1879 a group of men interested in seeing the area reach a greater potential formed the West End Association.

In November of that year Edward Clark described his vision for the future of the area to the Association's members, and the following February those members met to consider the future of what was thought to be the area's most impressive boulevard, then known as Eighth Avenue, but now called Central Park West. Most of the people there favored renaming it West Central Park, but Edward Clark, then at least six months from starting any work on the Dakota, was opposed. He said that he thought the West Side avenues should be named "after such of the states as have well-sounding names."

Clark had previously built the Van Corlear apartments – the name a reference to a prominent early Dutch family – but would soon demonstrate an affection for American Indian and Western associations, constructing two smaller apartment buildings, the Wyoming and the Ontiora, in addition to the Dakota. "The names of the newest states and territories have been chosen with excellent taste," he said, and suggested Montana Place for Eighth Avenue, Wyoming Place for Ninth Avenue, Arizona Place for Tenth Avenue, and Idaho Place for Eleventh Avenue. His colleagues were deaf to his all-American suggestion, West End Avenue was christened in 1880 and Central Park West received its name in 1883, leaving Ninth and Tenth Avenues intact.

In 1890, a group of property owners mobilized to re-label them Columbus and Amsterdam Avenues. The account of their reasons is revealing. Part of the rationale was that new names would distinguish the haut-bourgeois West Side from the lower part of the city through which the numbered avenues ran, particularly the undistinguished factories, flats, and tenements of the West 30s, 40s, and 50s. In September 1890, months after the change had been made, The *Real Estate Record & Guide* quoted an unidentified builder disdaining Central Park West and Amsterdam as too unwieldy to be taken up by the public; the only people who would use them being real estate agents.

A related move to establish the separate identity of the new neighborhood came in 1886, when the side street lots were renumbered beginning at Central Park West, instead of Fifth Avenue, so that the first building off Central Park West was No. 1 West, not No. 301 West.

For many years the Dakota has been conjured up as a wildly improbable venture, off in the wilds. Is that really the way it seemed to New Yorkers of the 1880s when it was built? Many popular guidebooks retell the well-known anecdote of the huge apartment building ridiculed for being so far out of town that it might as well have been in the Dakotas. Both the name and the myth stuck. This amusing story is devotedly repeated in scores of guidebooks and supposedly authoritative histories. That it always appears without a source, without variation or elaboration, and without the flavor of real life apparently never raised anyone's suspicions. Or perhaps they just liked the myth and didn't want to dispute the source. And while it is true that when the Dakota was built there was little in its immediate area, that "little" included the American Museum of Natural History, the fast elevated trains running up what is now Columbus Avenue, and several score of row houses.

However, everyone agreed on the great prospects for the area: The El made commuting downtown from the West Side faster than by surface transit from much farther south, and Central Park had been a major tourist attraction for a decade. Beyond the park, the East Side had largely filled up with row houses and apartment buildings, and the price of West Side real estate, especially along what is now Central Park West, had increased dramatically. West Side terra was hardly incognita, or even Dakota.

It is significant that, in the several dozen articles covering the construction of the building in the trade and popular press, not one remarks anything at all on the supposed remoteness of the area. The first publication of the name "Dakota" in the *Real Estate Record & Guide* of June 3, 1882, is straightforward and without evidence of any gibe. In fact, the first appearance of *any* story on how the Dakota got its name appears to have been not in the 19th century at all, but in an article that appeared in 1933 in the *New York Herald Tribune* that reported on a festive luncheon held in the Dakota private dining room to celebrate the 50th birthday of the building. George P. Douglass, who had been manager of the building since 1897, after the lunch was over gave the reporters in attendance a tour around the building and recounted its history. Even though he had known members of the family and staff of Edward Clark who were alive when the building went up and who might have given him first-hand reports, he said this about the building's name: "Probably it was called `Dakota' because it was so far west and so far north." For someone with his tenure at the building to present the story as a casual conjecture hardly provides the ring of authenticity.

FIG. 49. The first building of the American Museum of Natural History in 1877 *AMNH Negative #471*

FIG. 50. West from the Dakota roof showing rock removal from what by then was the property of young Edward Severin Clark, with the Ninth Avenue Elevated station at 72nd Street, and the Hudson River and New Jersey in the distance. Edward Clark's two sets of row houses are at the right. *Museum of the City of New York print archives 92.34.2*

FIG. 53. Northwest from the Dakota in 1887. Straight ahead is the American Museum of Natural History. At the left is the track of the Ninth Avenue Elevated running along Columbus Avenue. *American Museum of Natural History negative #326322*

Just how undeveloped was that part of the city when the Dakota was constructed? This much (figs 50, 51, 52, 53, and 54).

FIG. 51. Southwest from the Dakota c.1886 showing the 72nd Street station of the Ninth Avenue elevated railway with the Hudson River and New Jersey beyond. *New York Public Library*

FIG. 52. South from the Dakota in 1887. At the upper left are the buildings of the Central Park Apartments or Spanish Flats, and to their right, the back of the Osborne at 57th Street and Seventh Avenue. *H.B.Jackson, New-York Historical Society negative #7274c*

FIG. 54. Northeast from the Dakota in 1887. A turreted row house is on 81st Street just to the right of the Museum building. A long row of houses in under construction on 82nd Street, Central Park West is at the right. The sign on the small building at the northwest corner of 75th Street reads Ale & Lager Beer Depot. Note the neatly built stone wall along the north side of 74th Street in the foreground. *Museum of the City of New York print archives 92.34.3*

FIG. 55. A woodcut accompanying a long article about the building in the 10 September 1884 issue of *The Daily Graphic* reporting on the completed Dakota.

# CHAPTER 6

# Apartment floor plans
# leading up to the Dakota

NTIL WELL AFTER the end of the Civil War, there were few available housing alternatives. Even in dense urban centers like New York, the one-family private house was the norm for those who could afford it. Poor people lived in converted houses or purpose-built tenements, and lower-middle-class folk relied on boarding houses and hotels. The first middle-class apartment house that opened in 1870 presented a wholly new alternative way of living.

Although the Stuyvesant was designed by the accomplished architect Richard Morris Hunt and well financed by its wealthy young developer Rutherfurd Stuyvesant, as an initial experiment it understandably had many shortcomings.

The elements of the plan that set it clearly apart from a common tenement were: a separate dining room; a kitchen remote from the rest of the apartment; provision for a live-in servant; a separate service stair; and a dumbwaiter for the delivery of coal and ice and the removal of ashes and garbage (implying there was staff in the building to operate it). On the less desirable side of the ledger, the rooms were not large, there was only a single bathroom, remote from the two front bedrooms, the inner hallway was contorted, and there was no elevator (fig. 56).

Finished in 1876, The Albany, on the west side of Broadway, from 52nd to 53rd Streets, was considerably larger, but did little to alleviate the problems inherent in the Stuyvesant. Indeed, it introduced additional problems. Because it had a much longer exposure to the street, more outside windows were possible, but the rooms that didn't enjoy this amenity looked out on narrow courtyards, or in many cases on tiny air shafts, which were not fitted with any mechanical ventilation. Secondary internal stairs were provided for each apartment, rising from the basement with dumbwaiters within each, but there still was no elevator, and room sizes were still minimal (fig. 57). But perhaps worst, from the point of view of socially-conscious tenants, was the presence of stores on the ground floor, a common feature of tenement houses for the lower classes and one that introduced a problem of how the apartments would be perceived. Appearances were very important in the latter part of the 19th century, so the architect, John C. Babcock attempted to ameliorate this by placing the entrances to the apartment building on the side streets, as far away from the stores as feasible. It was clear that improvements in planning and construction would have to be made before the concept of an apartment house would be a practical or appealing alternative for those seeking a comfortable living style and a socially acceptable situation.

Completed in the same year as The Albany, the first Osborne on Fifth Avenue north of 52nd Street was designed by architects Duggin & Crossman (fig. 58). For a building erected at the dawn

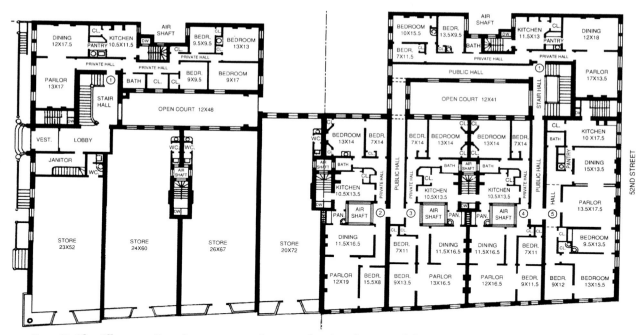

Fig. 57. The Albany on Broadway, 51st-52nd streets showing the ground floor at the left and a typical upper floor at the right.

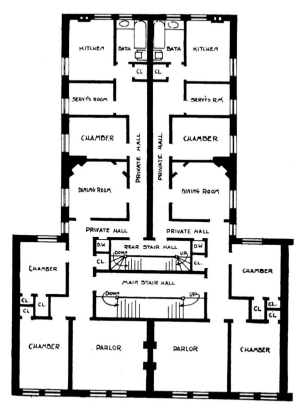

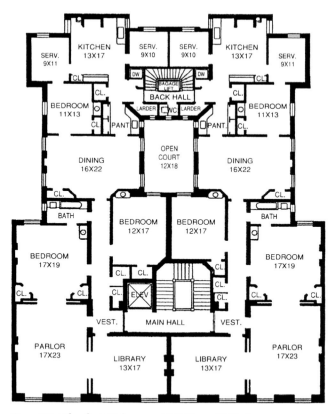

Fig. 56. Typical half-floor of the Stuyvesant Apartments at 142 East 18 Street, designed by Richard Morris Hunt in 1869 and built by Rutherfurd Stuyvesant

Fig. 58. The first Osborne of 1876, on Fifth Avenue

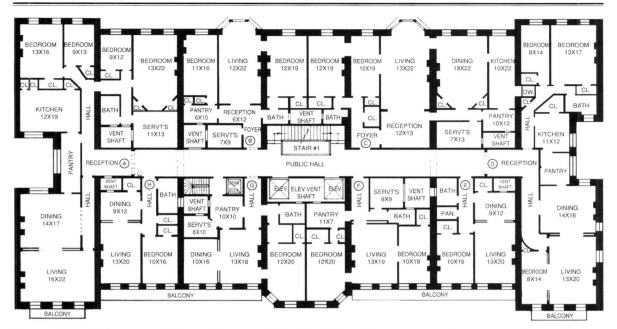

FIG. 59. The Chelsea at 222 West 23 Street as originally built in 1883 as a cooperative apartment house. It became a hotel in 1905

of the apartment age, it had a creditable plan that included a front stairway and passenger elevator, as well as a back stairway and a baggage lift. Each of the two apartments per floor was provided with a dumbwaiter for delivery of packages, a chute for the removal of ashes, and a toilet in the back hallway for the use of the servants (although no separate servant's bathroom). Indeed, each apartment had but a single bathroom (without a sink), although each of the three bedrooms had its own sink. Curious by our standards, one of the bedrooms was only accessible from the dining room, and the largest one was connected by sliding double doors to the parlor. Similar doors connected the parlor to a library. This plan was a major improvement over what other developers of the period were producing, but it was within only a 75-foot-wide interior lot, and provided a total of only ten apartment units. It remained for the Dakota to set the much higher standards in a few years.

A much larger and rather different experimental example of apartment house planning was the Chelsea, erected as a cooperative venture where the majority of the tenants would together own the building. As originally designed, the building had about 100 units, 70 owned by stockholders. The remaining units were rented out, along with shops on the ground floor, thereby significantly reducing the monthly maintenance costs for the owners. Architects Hubert Pirsson & Company included a wide range of accommodations (fig. 59). The building could provide expansive units with large living and dining rooms, kitchens, multiple bedrooms, and servants' rooms, as well a smaller units without kitchens or dining rooms, for those who preferred to take their meals in the restaurant that had been constructed on the ground floor, adjoining the lobby and ladies' reception room. An unusual feature was top-floor apartments that were duplexed via internal stairways to extra-high studios at the roof level. Also on the roof was a garden and promenade for the common use of all residents of the building and their guests. It was suitably furnished, and offered exceptionally expansive views in all directions, as The Chelsea was the tallest apartment house in the city. The concept of cooperative living embodied in the scheme devised by Phillip Hubert for the Chelsea had its origins in an experiment in the 1840s in Rochdale, England where a group of farmers banded together in an attempt (ultimately partially successful) to deal with the financial problems of farming. This was an essentially socialistic idea of people working together for their common good by combining their resources with the goal of improving some aspect of their own lives rather than for the capitalistic goal of making a profit. It appears in various guises, the most pervasive one in Manhattan being the cooperative apartment house. The benefits of the cooperative scheme gives residents collective control over all the aspects of how the building is operated that are the bailiwick of the owner of a rental property. For a rental building, the interests of the tenants are essentially in opposition to those of the landlord, but in a cooperative there is an alignment of interests because collectively the tenants are also the landlord. Again and again this is evident when a rental building that has become run-down is converted to cooperative ownership. Because the owners are then those who live there, there is a strong incentive for restoring and upgrading the building. Other forces were at work at the Chelsea, resulting it its conversion from a cooperative apartment house to a hotel a little more than two decades after it was built.

Completed in 1881, the Windermere has always been considered a single apartment house, but it is in fact three separate buildings, each filed under a separate application to the Department of Buildings in 1881, and each obviously designed as a self-contained unit (fig. 60). The section at 408 West 57 Street offered two units per floor, with an elevator. There was a separation of the kitchen and dining room from the rest of each apartment, but this placed the single bathroom far from the bedrooms. The planning was primitive; to get from the living room to the dining room one had to go out into the public hall, or go through the master bedroom, and the three additional bedrooms all opened onto tiny air shafts. Similarly poor planning is evidenced in the walk-up section at 404 West 57 Street, featuring single units per floor. After construction had been completed, the apartments on the sixth and seventh floors were declared to be illegal because too many flights of stairs were required to reach them. So they were annexed to the adjacent apartments in 400 West 57 Street, resulting

FIG. 60. The three buildings of the Windermere Apartments on West 57th Street

in huge, contorted, and un-rentable apartment units. Even though the rooms in it were larger, and more enjoyed outside exposure, the corner building overlooked the Ninth Avenue elevated railway, a noisy detriment for which the provision of a passenger elevator and a service lift was hardly compensation. Although aimed originally at an upper-middle-class tenancy, the inept planning by its architects, Theophilus G. Smith and Nathaniel A. McBride, meant that its units couldn't be rented as complete apartments at levels sufficient for an adequate return on its investment, so very early in its life it was subdivided for single-room occupancy, with the renters of the individual rooms sharing joint bathroom and kitchen facilities. Although in designating the Windermere as a landmark, the New York City Landmarks Preservation Commission claimed that it represented "luxury housing," the Windermere in fact represented a dead end for apartment house planning.

Among the first truly luxury apartment houses in the city was the Van Corlear. What made it so was not so much the materials used, which were substantial and of fine quality, but the overall planning, the details the building provided, and how it accomplished its aims. This suggests that there was a very close collaboration between the developer Clark and his architect Hardenbergh. Clark was not a speculative builder leveraging his cash to increase his profit and with every decision aimed at maximizing a return-on-investment (as evidently so with most other apartment developers). Rather, he was a mature businessman who had established a long-term cash flow by developing and perfecting a new product (a mass-market sewing machine) and then creating a widespread perceived need for that product, thereby further increasing that cash flow. It appears that his mind worked in a similar way in developing and perfecting the concept of a large, luxury apartment house, although his death in 1882 prevented him from maximizing its market. Clark had already developed several architectural projects in upstate New York with Hardenbergh, suggesting that they had developed a good working relationship, and that the Van Corlear (and later the Dakota) was the product of their joint efforts. This presumed symbiotic rapport makes it difficult to assign credit to either man for any of the specifics that made both these buildings so successful.

A comparison of the typical floor plan of the Van Corlear (fig. 61) with the later typical floor plan at the Dakota (fig. 62) reveals a number of ways in which the Van Corlear served as the testing ground for the larger building. Most obvious is the full-block coverage of both buildings with a single large rectangular courtyard in the middle to replace multiple small vent shafts typical of the plans used by most contemporary architects. Second is the service ramp at the side leading down to the basement level, the difference being that the Dakota arrangement improved on the earlier one by providing an enclosed lower courtyard for the service and delivery vehicles, reserving the open upper courtyard solely for the carriages of the residents and their guests. In both buildings, the boiler room was placed in a separate structure outside the walls of the apartment house. Although there were of course boiler explosions from time to time, actual safety appears to have been secondary to the appearance of safety. At the time the Van Corlear was erected, apartment houses were still looked upon with considerable disfavor by middle- and upper-class people, for both social and practical reasons. To many, they were simply tenement houses in fancy clothing. And tenements were often fire traps. Developers of apartment houses attempted to allay such fears by installing (and touting in their promotional advertising) fire alarm systems, fire-proof hallways and stairs, and multiple means of escape. The way the heating system was installed and operated was of considerable inter-

FIG. 61. The 1879 Van Corlear on Seventh Avenue from 55th to 56th Streets with the ground floor to the right and a typical upper floor to the left. Each side of the building has its own side-street entrance and three apartments per floor.

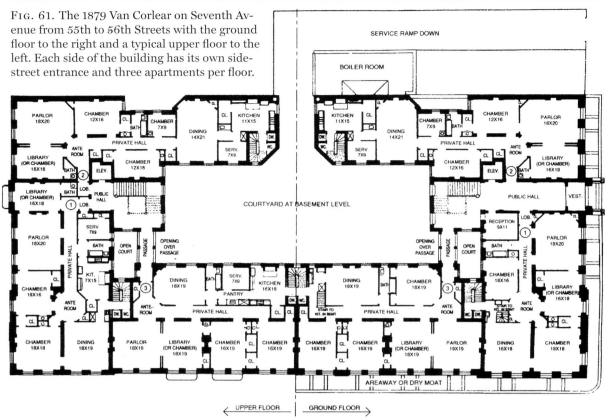

est to the potential apartment renter, so placing the dangerous equipment outside the limits of the building. where it could do less damage if it exploded, helped instill confidence. At the Van Corlear, the boilers would have been relatively small, so they could fit into a modestly-sized ancillary building adjacent to the apartment house and accessible via the service ramp for the delivery of coal. At the Dakota, a far larger building requiring greater heating capacity, a larger structure was required. But Edward Clark also wanted to provide an electrical generating plant to provide power and lighting not only to his new apartment house, but also to the many rowhouses he was building nearby. As he held those houses for rental, rather than selling them, he was concerned with ongoing maintenance and utility supplies. Accordingly, he constructed a large boiler and dynamo structure adjacent to the Dakota, placing it entirely underground, while creating a small park at grade level. Later, after the Edison Electric Company extended service to the area and the dynamos became redundant, and improvements to boilers made them safer, the heating and other service equipment was relocated to the basement of the Dakota, and the adjoining underground structure was removed. Another way that architect Hardenbergh distinguished the Van Corlear (and later the Dakota) from ordinary tenement houses was by providing one set of elevators and stairways for residents and a second set for tradesmen and service purposes.

An unusual feature at the Van Corlear was the aerial entrance passageways that served to connect apartment number 3 on each floor with the public stair hall and elevator landing. By giving them lower ceiling heights and leaving the space open above and below them, air flow was maintained to the windows beyond them, thereby allowing the passages to span the corners

FIG. 62. Early floor plan with dining room accessible only from within the building.

of the courtyard without unduly intruding upon them or defeating the purposes of that large open space. Hardenbergh used a similar device at the Dakota to connect one of the two apartments at the north side of each floor to the single service elevator and stair tower on that side of the building. A full-height open slot connected the central courtyard with the outside air at 73rd Street, and as windows opened onto that slot, it had to be maintained. By using low-ceilinged aerial connecting passageways (with open air both above and below each one), he was able to accomplish that goal while still providing the necessary access to the service tower (fig. 63).

Designed and constructed after the Van Corlear, but contemporaneously with the Dakota, the Osborne was the second apartment house to carry that name, in this case more logically, as it was the name of its builder, Thomas Osborne, a stone contractor. Osborne understood the inherent luxury of fine materials and made lavish use of them constructing his building, so much so that he went bankrupt before the building was completed. Although Osborne lost his building, it was completed, opened, and well received by the public. While the rich design of the interiors doubtless helped, of probably greater importance was the functionality of the apartments themselves. Designed by James E. Ware, who was better known for working-class tenements, the planning arrangement made use of a device that had been pioneered by Hubert & Pirsson in some of their Home Clubs (but not the Chelsea). For the Osborne, Ware provided extra floors with lower ceiling heights at the back for bedrooms, contrasting with the higher-ceilinged entertainment rooms at the front. This entailed a complex system of half-flights of stairs and interlocking floors that required multiple floor plans to describe adequately, but which worked admirably to yield a greater total number of rooms and square footage. As can be seen in the accompanying plan (fig. 64), the room sizes and arrangements of the apartments themselves were well done, but the use of the site resulted in light courts with little light and no views. Although the Van Corlear had been completed by the time Osborne and Ware were preparing the Osborne plans, it is clear the superior planning skills of Henry Hardenbergh were lost on them.

FIG. 63. Aerial connecting passageways at the Dakota *Michael Garrett*

Built at about the same time as the Dakota and the Osborne was the eight-building complex generally referred to as the Spanish Flats (after the names of the individual buildings) or the Navarro (after the name of its original developer). The overall planning of the project included ramp-accessed below-grade provision for delivery wagons, just as the Van Corlear and the Dakota did, but the layouts of the apartments were far from convenient for either the resident families or their servants (fig. 65). The three-against-two arrangement of the service floors meant that in most cases food had to be carried up or down stairs to get from kitchen to dining room, and the minimal bathroom facilities (generally one to an apartment, for up to five bedrooms) were similarly up or down half a flight of stairs, and a long trek from some of those bedrooms. The materials and fitments of the Navarro apartments may have been lavish, but the planning of the units was far from the modern concept of luxurious.

Because the original construction drawings and other documents for the Dakota are lost, we can rely only on published plans and descriptions to tell us how the project was originally conceived and how it developed. The transactions for 1882-1883 of the Royal Institute of British Architects tell something of the project and provide this plan for the first floor, including a restaurant and café available to the general public through direct street access (fig. 66). Although this was later changed so that the dining room would be for the residents and their guests only, the plan can extrapolated to suggest that originally there were to be six apartments to a floor, the same as at the Van Corlear. As at the earlier building, a very large internal courtyard is evident with only two air shafts, solely to bathrooms and servants' rooms. Not appearing in this plan is the service ramp at the west side of the building down to a service court directly beneath the residents' court at the ground floor, as well as the separate boiler house on the adjacent property, both features first found at the Van Corlear. The unique brilliance of this original Dakota plan (followed in all the essentials by the final one as built) is evident. In retrospect it is perhaps too easy for us in the 21st century, for whom luxury apartment living is seemingly embedded in our DNA, to forget that in the 1870s is was still a new frontier, undefined and not even a concept secure in the abstract. What was wanted and what was provided in a

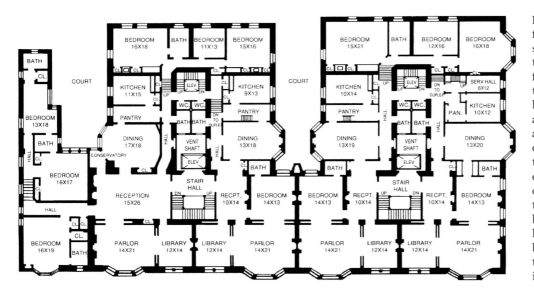

FIG. 64. A version of the floor plan of the Osborne showing the bedrooms in the back that are a partial flight of stairs up from their front rooms; the back bedrooms for two of the apartments in this plan are a partial flight of stairs down and are underneath the bedrooms that appear on the plan. For two floors of entertaining rooms, there were three floors of bedrooms. This yielded lower ceiling heights in the bedrooms, but increased the total area of the building on the site.

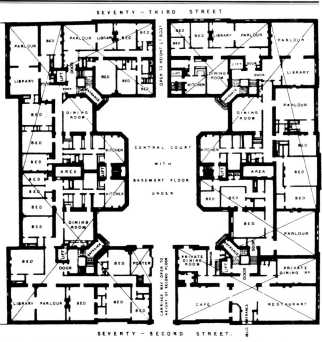

FIG. 65. Two adjoining apartments in the Spanish Flats at the corner of Seventh Avenue and 59th Street.

FIG. 66. Early unbuilt arrangement of Dakota first floor with public access to the restaurant directly from the street. The six apartments planned for this floor are each crossed to show their extent and size.

tenement house was generally understood, yet even that was a far cry from what we today consider the essentials of housing to which every American is entitled. If tenement housing needs (which had existed for 2000 years) weren't yet fully developed, how then could anyone even imagine the needs of luxury apartment housing – a concept not even ten years old. What was being provided in upper-class brownstone row houses was known, and in fact the interiors of the apartments in the Dakota and of other lesser apartment houses superficially and deliberately imitated those of rowhouses. But the unknown area of experimentation was in what single-family houses by their very nature were incapable of providing. Second-guessing the market by deciding where to spend money on the new product and where not to was what separated the successful ventures from those that failed. Finding the sweet spot was the trick. Luxury designs and finishes, but not too much. Large rooms, but not too large. A balance in the provision of bedrooms, bathrooms, servants' rooms, and support spaces. Spacious circulation but not too expansive. Adequate closets and storage, but not wasteful. Dependable technology, and perhaps most important, personal privacy for individual family members and the staff. Clearly, Clark was applying to the upper-class housing market the same sort of innovative thinking he had used for the middle-class market for sewing machines. On multiple fronts he was devising a better product and figuring out how to create a market for that product. The concept of "life style housing" wasn't invented the day-before-yesterday. Edward Clark and Henry Hardenbergh succeeded admirably in bringing all the pieces together and making them work smoothly. The result is the remarkable record of an apartment house that has provided a container for luxurious living to a small segment of very wealthy New Yorkers for more than 130 years. Edward Clark and Henry Hardenbergh planned it, and planned it well.

Fɪɢ. 67. The Dakota entrance in a 1974 lithograph © Richard Haas, licensed by VAGA, New York, NY, *courtesy of Robert K. Newman, www.OldPrintShop.com.*

# CHAPTER 7

# Construction of the Dakota

I N PLANNING and building the Dakota, Edward Clark had several clear advantages over all other developers of New York apartment houses. For starters, he was using his own money. He had no partners, no borrowed money or mortgages, and he owned the land on which he was building. He also had a great deal of available cash to draw on as the project progressed. And while his stated goal in initiating the venture was to make money, it is clear that his real estate activities in the city were intended to create a long term revenue stream for his grandchildren, rather than any conventional investor's immediate return-on-investment.

But perhaps of far greater importance was Clark's lifetime record of business experience in creating value outside the box. Clark hadn't made his money merely by being a lucky (or even shrewd) investor in an established field. He did it by imaginatively creating an entirely new market for products he could produce better than anyone else. And he accomplished that by being a very observant evaluator of people and how they interacted with the elements of their lives. He was able to imagine what their lives were lacking, and thereby to create desires that people never imagined that they had. Instead of looking for existing needs to fulfill with an existing product, he created them. And he did so on a huge scale with complete confidence and self-assurance. When he applied those insights to his Singer sewing machines and the middle-class market for them, he made a huge fortune. For the Dakota it was upper-class housing accommodations at a palatial level of luxury, set in a newly-developing Upper West Side whose potential for long term growth was not completely obvious to those with conventional vision.

The Van Corlear was the testing ground for the Dakota's planning. It had used the French concept of a large internal courtyard with access from the street for deliveries, but for the Dakota, Clark and Hardenbergh (Clark was very much a hands-on entrepreneur) took the courtyard, enlarged it significantly, and expanded it to two levels, thereby echoing the traditional upstairs/downstairs separation of family and servants in single-family rowhouse living. They expanded on the second staircase that was originally only for fire safety, and turned it into a completely separate service stair for the apartments' kitchens, a second function to the fire-emergency one. In place of small dumbwaiters for deliveries and garbage removal, the Dakota provided full-sized service elevators devoted to freight plus servants and tradesmen.

The Van Corlear apartment layouts had given thought to a separation of the three basic functions of apartment living – entertaining, sleeping, and service – but it wasn't quite as successful as it might have been. For the Dakota, greater space and greater thought yielded more functional arrangements in each apartment. The building itself similarly separated service spaces from living areas for tenants. The eighth and ninth floors originally contained only laundry rooms, sleeping and bathroom facilities for servants (both resident and visiting), with spaces on the tenth floor or roof level for children's play areas, laundry drying facilities, and water tanks for domestic supply and to operate the hydraulic elevators.

Those elevators were amenities designed to enhance the luxury of the building. In the original planning, enough were supplied to allow each to serve only two apartments. Their operation was silent, smooth, secure, and sedately slow. And their disposition was part of the planning approach that Clark took for the entire building. He recognized that he had to create an entirely new concept of luxury living that would make the apartments he offered even more attractive than conventional brownstones. What he aimed to achieve was expansive and personal intimacy enclosed by palatial grandeur. The apartments would be larger and internally more convenient than the typical brownstone. Reaching each apartment's front door from the street would be almost as private and convenient as reaching a brownstone's entry and that entry would look the same. Inside, the aesthetics of the each apartment would be recognizable to brownstone owners. The moldings, woodwork, fireplace mantels, ceiling heights, flooring, hardware, and fixtures, would all be familiar, although the fittings in the kitchens and bathrooms would present the top-of-the-line latest designs and technology. But the apartment would be part of a palatial residence that would be larger and grander than what even the richest tenants might be able to afford individually. This wasn't merely a set of specifications for an apartment building. This was a marketing concept for an entirely new way of living for those with the wherewithal to afford it. An ambitious brief, but one on which Hardenbergh delivered.

The basic planning for the building itself is essentially that of a hollow square, 204 feet 4 inches along Central Park West and 200 feet along 72nd and 73rd Streets, with an H-shaped central courtyard (fig. 51). Generally speaking, the original plan was for eight apartments per floor. Two apartments would share one passenger elevator and open staircase, those four vertical circulation towers being in the corners of the courtyard, accessed at the ground floor. Residents and guests on foot or in their carriages would enter the courtyard through a grand arched and vaulted entry on 72nd Street. From there, short stairways from the corners of the courtyard provided access to each of the four small entrance lobbies. There is also secondary vertical circulation in the form of four service elevators and service stairways, again each serving two apartments.

There is a secondary entrance to the courtyard from 73rd Street, which before long was closed off and used only for the entrance and departure of funeral participants. A service driveway was provided from the two side streets down to the basement level, where a lower level of the courtyard could be accessed. Where residents' carriages could enter and turn around in the ground-floor courtyard, the carts and delivery wagons of tradesmen and service people could do the same in the basement-level service court, lit by two circular skylights contained within a pair of decorative fountains at the street level around which the carriages could turn.

Evidently, many potential tenants wanted modifications to the initial apartment layouts, so the plans were modified to accommodate them. This resulted in a significantly different mix of apartment sizes and arrangements from that first contemplated. At some point it was decided to modify the second floor to provide small self-contained apartments and separate rooms for guests, in addition to several regular fully-equipped apartments similar to those on the higher floors. Much later, many of the extra servants' and laundry rooms on the eighth and ninth floors were converted to small apartments as well.

The private dining facilities on the first floor comprised a large dining room, a smaller private dining room, and a separate parlor or reception room. Kitchen and service spaces for the food operation were provided be in the basement, with a stair and dumbwaiter connection. The dining operation (including meals provided to residents for consumption in their own apartments) remained until after World War II. Eventually, the space devoted to the food service was sold as shares of the cooperative apartment corporation and was converted to a living and gallery space for artist Giora Novak, who used the former kitchen spaces in the basement as his studio.

The land under the Dakota was originally Lots 25-40 of Block 1125, later combined and numbered Lot 25. That property was bought by Edward Clark on 31 December 1877 from August and Caroline Belmont under a deed recorded in Liber 1443, page 307. According to the records of the Department of Buildings, the plans and specifications for the new building were officially submitted on 29 September 1880 and were approved on 6 October 1880, although doubtless the details and scope of the project had been discussed (and perhaps negotiated) with the building officials for weeks before. Construction was begun on 25 October 1880 and completed on 27 October 1884 (fig. 68). The owner was listed as Edward Clark, Esq., 34 Union Square,. and the architect as H.J. Hardenbergh, 111 Broadway. The builder was John Banta, who had facilities at 198 Broadway, and on West 17th Street, and who lived at 294 West 4th Street. The superintendent of construction for the owner was George Henry Griebel, who worked in a similar capacity on other projects for the Clark estate for many years after.

The specifications were given as follows: Depth of foundation walls from the curb level to be "from 10 to 18 feet," that foundation to be set "on solid rock," with its walls to be "from 3 to 4 feet" thick, constructed of "blue stone laid in cement mortar." Floors were "to have rolled beams from 6 to 12 ins. deep," with "beams on all floors to be from 3 to 4 feet apart," with floors to be "arched in brick or terra cotta." Partitions surrounding the public halls were to be of "fireproof blocks." All other partitions either of brick or fireproof blocks." The exterior walls of the first story were to be "24 to 28 inches;" second through fourth stories, "20 to 24 inches;" fifth and sixth stories, "16 to 20 inches;" above sixth story, "12 to 16 inches." The stair-

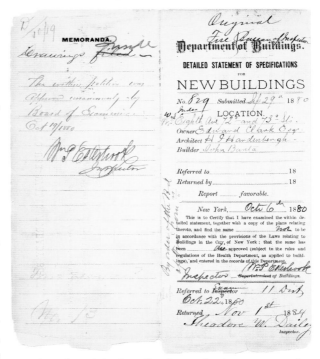

FIG. 68. The original application to the Department of Buildings for the construction of the Dakota

cases were to be fireproof and constructed of iron, with the main stairs having marble treads. The elevator shafts were to be "all enclosed in brick." The stated occupancy was to be as a "Family Hotel," with apartments for 42 families besides janitors. There were to be six families on each floor, with "a part of building on 1st floor and basement to be used as a public restaurant – janitors families in basement." The estimated construction cost was given as "about $1,000,000.00" That would be about $24,000,000 today.

On 9 October 1880, about two weeks before construction was to begin, the *Real Estate Record & Guide* published an article describing what was then believed would be a residential hotel, doubtless based on the intended occupancy as stated on the building application. While we think of a hotel as having one- or two-room suites, this so-called family hotel would have suites from five to twenty rooms, and there would be between forty and fifty of them. (See Appendix H for the complete article).

The *Real Estate Record and Builders Guide* periodically reported on the building project. In the issue for 8 October 1881 they had this to say:

> The great apartment house of Mr. Edward Clark on Eighth avenue between Seventy-second and Seventy-third streets, is now up to the second story. As, however, this magnificent structure is to be eight stories in height, it is hardly to be expected that it will be under roof before the winter sets in. There is to be good, honest work on this building, which cannot be hurried. It is understood that Mr. Clark intends to erect a fine clutch of buildings on Seventy-third street. They are to be first class dwellings. Rumor has it that the whole block bounded by Eighth and Ninth avenues, Seventy-third and Seventy-fourth streets is to be built upon by Mr. Clark. Half a dozen capitalists, like Mr. Clark, would soon work a marvelous change on the West Side.

Two weeks later on 22 October 1881 that journal commented on a particular aspect of the project:

### ARTESIAN WELLS IN NEW YORK

> Just at this time, when the scarcity of Croton water is making itself felt, it is well to remember that we are not entirely dependent upon it for our supply. There are a number of artesian wells in this city that yield a supply of good water, and there should be more of them. Good water and plenty of it, is what our people demand and will have. The waste of water is criminal, but the free use of it should not be interfered with. Many of our large breweries are supplied with artesian wells, as well as some of our hotels and Turkish bathing establishments. Mr. Edward Clark is setting a good example to the builders of large apartment houses by boring an artesian well at the rear of his new mammoth family hotel on Eighth avenue. On last Saturday it had reached a depth of 365 feet, and was 8 inches in diameter, the water coming from two veins. He has also an artesian well in the rear of the Van Corlear apartment house, 275 feet deep and 7 inches in diameter, which, when it is not in use, is a flowing well. The water in these wells can be used for all household purposes, and in fact it is thought to be equal if not superior to Croton for all uses. It is said that unless we have a fall of rain, the supply of water in the Fifth avenue Reservoir will be totally exhausted within the coming three weeks.

In the issue of 25 March 1882, a perennial problem at construction sites was described:

> Work on the great apartment house on Eighth avenue is to be suspended, it is reported, on account of the extravagant demands of the bricklayers and other laborers heretofore employed. Nor will the erection of the proposed thirty-eight houses on Seventy-third street be commenced this spring by Mr. Clark if the workmen persist in demanding increased wages. The RECORD was the first to announce the stoppage of work on the new opera house and the hotel on the corner of Broadway and Thirty-ninth

street. It is to be regretted that anything would put a stop to building operations in this city. The growth of our population and business demand increased accommodations, and laborers hurt themselves in many ways by asking too much. It advances their own house rents, for less tenements are erected, a fact that the landlord takes advantage of to advance the price of his apartments. It is to be hoped that some satisfactory basis will be arrived at between builders and those they employ, so that the work of building up the city can keep right on.

The *Real Estate Record and Builders Guide* had been publishing a series of critical articles on apartment houses, and in the issue for 21 October 1882 they described and reviewed the Dakota's architectural appearance.

The latest, the largest, and the costliest of the apartment houses is thus far the most successful architecturally. This is the "Dakota," in Eighth avenue, extending from Seventy-second to Seventy-third streets, and about the same distance to the rear, so as to make it nearly a square of 200 feet. Mr. Hardenbergh is the architect, and he has had the benefit of the experience of previous designers of apartment houses, including his own – an experience which has certainly not been lost upon him. The building encloses a large court, visible from the outside through a narrow opening in the north wall, and consists, architecturally, of three fronts, one on each street and one on the avenue. The problem of securing repose without monotony and animation without restlessness, in so large a building was not an easy one, but it has been solved. Each front is treated in a manner by itself, so that none is the repetition of another, but there is not difference enough to interfere with the unity of the total impression from any point of view. Thus the north side has two gables near the centre, the east front two gables at the ends, the south front one gable at the centre, over the large archway which is the principal entrance. Each wall is distinctly divided into beginning, middle and end. A basement of two stories, the openings of the first square headed, and of the second round arched, is separated by a broad and decorated band of light stone or terra cotta from the main wall, which consists of four stories treated nearly alike. Then comes a shell frieze of terra cotta and over this a narrow balcony upon which the windows of the seventh story open, while there is an eighth story in the roof itself. Not the least attraction of the building is its color – yellow or rather salmon colored brick from Perth Amboy with olive sandstone from Nova Scotia, a combination almost unique here and very agreeable. The stone is used in quoins at the angles of the projecting masses crowned by the gables, in the coping of these gables, in the arches and jambs of the openings and in belt courses. There are besides two well designed oriels in stone, curved in plan, each running through six stories on the south side. The expression of the building, as we have said, is at once sober and animated, and this expression is heightened by the skill and restraint with which the detail is designed. This is, in the main, a reminiscence of French Renaissance, used with freedom and intelligence. There are, naturally, drawbacks to the complete success of the building. The detail, never offensive or extravagant, is here and there flat and thin, notably in the main entrance, which sadly lacks depth, and it is sometimes irrationally applied, as in an overlaying of "architecture" upon the uppermost story of the east front, which projects beyond the plane of the wall below. The architect must regret, now that he sees the work in place, that he permitted himself to diversify one story of his oriels with meaningless pilasters, and it is questionable whether he ought not to regret that he did not still further emphasize the division of the beginning of his building from the middle, by making the whole basement of stone. The projections of the gabled pavilions are too shallow to be fully effective; and indeed, we might sum up the shortcomings of this building by saying that it lacks depth and force of modeling. But these are shortcomings only, be it noted, in the expression of an idea and the execution of an architectural design, upon the success of which, in spite of the shortcomings, the architect of the "Dakota" is to be heartily congratulated.

On 5 April 1884, the *Real Estate Record and Builder's Guide* reported that the building was almost finished.

> The "Dakota" is at last near completion, and is receiving its finishing touches prior to its opening in May, when it will be quite ready for dwelling purposes. This huge structure is ten stories and basement in height, and has a total frontage of over 600 feet, 204.4 feet on the avenue and 200 feet on both Seventy-second and Seventy-third street. It contains fifty-six suites of apartments, with two to twenty rooms in each, there being about five hundred rooms in all. It is expected that when the building is fully occupied that some three thousand people will reside in it including the army of servants and other auxiliaries. The material is of brick and Nova Scotia stone. A novel feature will be that the building will be lighted throughout by electricity, supplied by a machine of 600 horse power. This will communicate also with the row of buildings belonging to the Clark estate on the north side of Seventy-third street, which will also contain electric lighting, being probably the first instance on record where the new light will be used for domestic purposes on so large a scale, there being some thirty houses in all. The building has eight Otis elevators, four passenger and four freight. The principal contractors are: John L. Banta, mason; T. Brien, plumber; Post & McCord, ironwork; J. L. Hamilton, carpenters; J. Gillis & Son and Henry Wilson, stonework; and Pottier & Stymus and others, woodwork. It may be interesting to note that the highest pinnacle on the "Dakota" is 185 feet. The architect is H. J. Hardenbergh, who states that the building when completed will have cost over $1,000,000.

Once the construction had been completed and the building opened, on 10 September 1884 *The Daily Graphic* published the first major article about the building, which was accompanied by a picture of the structure and a floor plan. It was hailed as "The Most Perfect Apartment House in the World." (See Appendix I for the complete text).

On 20 September 1884, the *Real Estate Record and Builder's Guide* revealed this under its "Gossip of the Week" column.

> The Dakota apartment house will be ready for occupancy October 1. The suites of apartments are renting at from $1,500 to $5,500 [per year]. There are fifty-eight sets of rooms, of which we are informed nearly twenty five percent are rented, mostly the lower-priced ones.

The *Real Estate Record and Builder's Guide* on 7 February 1884 published an article titled "How the Great Apartment Houses have Paid." Here is a portion of particular interest:

> The "Dakota" is ten stories high, eight of which are used for living purposes. It contains three frontages of 200 feet, on Eighth avenue, Seventy-second and Seventy-third streets. It contains fifty-eight suites of apartments and is estimated to have cost between $1,500,000 and $2,000,000, though the latter figure is probably nearer the mark. The rents range from $1,000 to $5,600. If entirely occupied, the rentals would yield $150,000 per annum. The running expenses amount to about $40,000, which would be increased to $50,000 or more if all the suites were occupied. At present, however, scarcely half have been rented. The net return on the cost of the building would be about 4 per cent, if all tenanted. Of course the "Dakota" may be regarded as an exception to the majority of apartment houses, as it was built not for speculation, nor to be disposed of at a large profit, nor with the object of being rented at high figures. The late Edward Clark had in view the erection of a noble structure, to be erected as an ornament to the west side, as well as for the accommodation of the affluent, and where architectural beauty was paramount, expense was ignored, with the result that the "Dakota" stands today unsurpassed amongst the apartment houses of the city. It may be added that the building is free from mortgage, is fire-proof, and insured at from fifteen to forty cents for three years. The architect was H. J. Hardenbergh.

The following year, on 7 March 1885, the *Real Estate Record & Guide* published a major report on the building, giving a detailed description of it and describing a tour that the reporter made of the entire building, from basement to roof. The conclusion was that it was "one of the noblest apartment houses of the world." (See Appendix J for the complete article).

FIG. 69. The north façade of the Dakota circa 1895, showing the completed Hotel Majestic to the south and the blockfront to the north that was then held vacant by the Clark family. *courtesy of the Office for Metropolitan History.*

F<small>IG</small>. 70. Perhaps the earliest known image of the Dakota, while still under construction. The Central Park statue of Daniel Webster, in bronze on a granite pedestal, was sculpted by Thomas Ball and erected in 1876, only four years before work on the Dakota was begun. *From a lantern slide, courtesy of Brian Merlis*

FIG. 71. A view of the Dakota from the West Drive within Central Park *"New York, 1894, Illustrated,"A.F. Parsons Publishing Co.*

FIG. 72. This image was made by a photographer sent by the Royal Institute of British Architects to create a record of modern architecture being built in New York. The picture probably dates to the Spring of 1884, as the rooms show no evidence of occupancy, and the pair of lighting stanchions has not yet been installed at the entrance. The many open windows suggest that final painting and varnishing may have been in progress.
*Royal Institute of British Architects RIBA 13670*

FIG. 73. A very early image, apparently before the site of the Hotel Majestic was offered for sale in 1889 (the For Sale sign that shows in the next photograph is lacking here). Two very small street lamps are in evidence, their size suggesting why the light stanchions flanking the building entrance are so grand and multi-headed. The multi-armed poles and telegraph and telephone wires evident in this photograph were gradually replaced by underground conduits following the infamous blizzard of 1888, which brought down thousands of poles, especially in the more congested sections of the city.
*New-York Historical Society negative #56312*

FIG. 74. An early photo of the Dakota. To the left in the background are some of the rowhouses that Clark built on the north side of 73rd Street east from Columbus Avenue in 1879-1880. In the left foreground is the site of the Hotel Majestic with a For Sale sign mounted behind the fence. Note the wooden telegraph poles and the iron rails set into 8th Avenue for the horse-drawn street-cars. There are no street signs, and no buildings yet evident north of the Dakota until 81st Street off in the distance. Hidden behind the Dakota, however, is the first section of the Museum of Natural History on 77th Street. *Museum of the City of New York Print Archives*

FIG. 75. The Dakota viewed from the Central Park access road about 1890, before the installation of the street lamps with their street signs along Central Park West, but the wooden telegraph poles have already been removed, doomed by The Great Blizzard of March 1888. The rustic shelters were original park features and surprisingly long-lived. The little sentry box dates to the time when the park was closed at night, and the iron gudgeons in the stone gate posts provided hooks to which chains could be attached to block off the park drives when the park was closed. No buildings had yet been constructed on 72nd Street. Off in the distance is a small apartment house on the far side of Columbus Avenue. *Museum of the City of New York 215853*

FIG. 76. In 1903 when this photograph was made, street lights and street signs had been installed. The building at the right is the southern section of the San Remo Hotel. The northern section was constructed first, with the later southern section filling the remainder of the block from 75th to 76th Streets, where the twin-towered San Remo apartment house now stands. Note that on the central gable on 72nd Street, a small dormer window, not visible in the prior photograph, has been installed near the ridge line. *A. Loeffler, Tompkinsville, New York*

FIG. 77. The photograph can be dated to about 1910 by the automobiles at the curb, and by the presence of the Langham Apartments at 135 Central Park West between 73rd and 74th Streets, which was completed in 1906. The sentry box for the guard has been replaced by a sign that warns visitors that "Any Person Taking Flowers or Leaves or defacing shrubbery in any Portion of the Park will be detained or Arrested and Punished." The central gable on 72nd Street has now gained another small dormer window, and the south side of the central gable on Central Park West has single one near the top as well. *Detroit Publishing Co. #043780*

FIG. 78. In this photo from 1924, The Langham apartment house is at the right, and at the left may be seen the fence and light fixture in front of the Hotel Majestic. The street lamps have gained large opaline glass globes to protect the lights, and the old small street signs have been replaced with the larger hump-backed versions that remained in use until late in the 20th century. There are two stanchions in the middle of the avenue with large cast-concrete white-painted bases that mark the stop for the trolley cars that continued to run along the avenue until the Independent Subway line opened about 1930. The large pair of lighting stanchions flanking the entrance driveway to the Dakota remain in place. They will not be replaced by the current building-mounted lanterns until the widening of 72nd Street's roadway (and narrowing of the sidewalks) required their removal as a traffic obstruction. *Wurts Brothers 806910, New-York Historical Society negative #56312*

FIG. 79. By 1961, when this photograph was taken around the time the building became a co-op, the entrance to the Eighth Avenue subway had been skillfully inserted into the moat area and the iron railing modified, but the stonework and brick walls had become decidedly dingy. It would be many years more before the building would be cleaned and by that time, the iconic Checker taxi cabs were no longer running. The building-mounted gas-fueled lanterns flanking the entrance archway were the replacements for the lighting stanchions on the sidewalk that had to be removed when the 72nd Street Roadway was widened. *Jack Boucher for the Historic American Buildings Survey*

FIG. 80. The west and south façades of the Dakota around 1894. The wooden fence surrounding the building's back yard has been replaced with an iron railing, and a pair of hedges has been planted to conceal the roof of the boiler house. Appearing immediately the left of the Dakota in the picture is the southwesterly corner on 74th Street of the original San Remo Hotel. *New York Public Library ID 1152565*

FIG. 81. The same view in 1961 after the external boilers and the later tennis courts were removed for car parking. The parking lot was later sold in connection with the sale of the Dakota to its tenants joining together as a cooperative corporation, and the Mayfair Tower apartments were built on the site at 15 West 72 Street. *Office for Metropolitan History*

FIG. 82. The west façade of the Dakota circa 1889. Removal of rock is underway to the west of the Dakota property. In the center of the lawn behind the apartment building is the roof of its underground boiler house, with a series of skylights or ventilators down the middle.
*Office for Metropolitan History*

FIGS. 83 & 84. The existing wall-mounted double gas lanterns flanking the entrance to the Dakota are not the original lighting that Henry Hardenbergh designed for the building. The putti-embellished urns are also not original, nor is the sentry box. When the building was new, there were no urns and no sentry box, and the lighting was provided by a pair of multi-armed lanterns on high cast-iron columns which in turn were mounted on high pedestal bases

FIGS. 85 & 86. Later, those lanterns gained central globes (probably to cast more light), were relocated to the curb (probably the better to spread that light), and were mounted on new larger pedestals. The original bases were refitted with the urns that are there now.

FIG. 87. Around the time that the lighting stanchions were put onto the larger bases by the curb, a sentry box was installed. It had a flat top and was apparently of wood.

FIG. 88. Finally, the stanchions at curbside were removed completely, doubtless when the 72nd Street roadway was widened. At that point, the wall-mounted gas lanterns were designed and installed, and the peak-topped metal sentry booth constructed.

FIG. 89. The original gates, locked at Midnight with an electric bell to ring for entry after that.

FIG. 90. Prior to 1891 when the Hotel Majestic was begun. The statue of Daniel Webster is still there.

FIG. 91. A colored flag would signal that the ice was thick enough to permit skating on the lake. The Dakota dominated the scene. *Shepp's New York City Illustrated*

FIG. 92. The Dakota at the left, probably in January or February of 1892. At the right is the first section of the Hotel San Remo. The southern section was built later that year. *Museum of the City of New York MNY 17631*

FIG. 93. After 1894 when the Hotel Majestic opened across the street. *Museum of the City of New York 25711*

FIG. 94. A postcard from c.1980

FIG. 95. A postcard mailed in 1907

FIG. 96. Development along Central Park West is proceeding with the erection of the 10-story Barnard apartments south of the Hotel Majestic. By 1906 the block from 70th to 71st Streets would be completed with the grandly luxurious Lorington. That block was dramatically changed less than 25 years later when 101 Central Park West was erected to replace them both. *Museum of the City of New York 215732*

Fɪɢ. 97. A pencil drawing over a tinted gesso base, by Richard Britell

# CHAPTER 8

# Floor plans of the Dakota and modern photographs

HE ORIGINAL architectural drawings for the Dakota have eluded discovery, as have any sketches or correspondence to indicate what changes were made to accommodate the wishes of early tenants, or the needs of the Clark family as owners or their building management. Nonetheless, many layout plans have surfaced over the years, including rental plans, and more recently, individual plans produced as aids for selling apartments. Based on all these sources, these new composite layouts have been drawn for all floors by architect Mia Ho. Dimensions are approximate, actual room usages may not agree with the nomenclature used here to identify the rooms, and positioning of walls and doors in some instances is speculative. Nonetheless, subject to those caveats, these floor plans provide a generally accurate idea of what the apartments in the Dakota are like today.

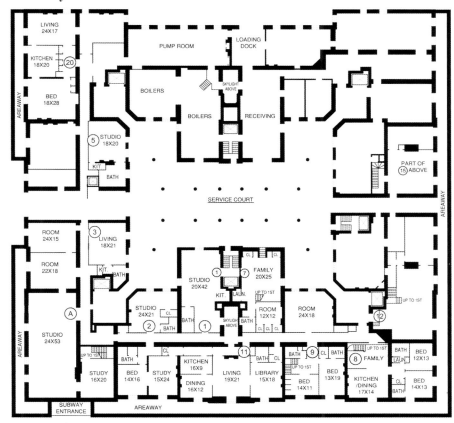

FIG. 98. BASEMENT

FIG. 99. FLOOR 1

FIG. 100. FLOOR 2

21 AND 22 ARE USED TOGETHER
AS A SINGLE APARTMENT

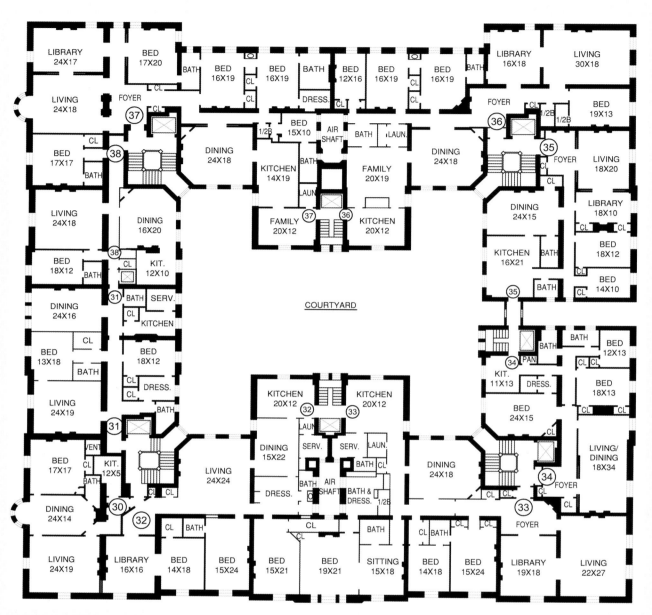

FIG. 101. FLOOR 3

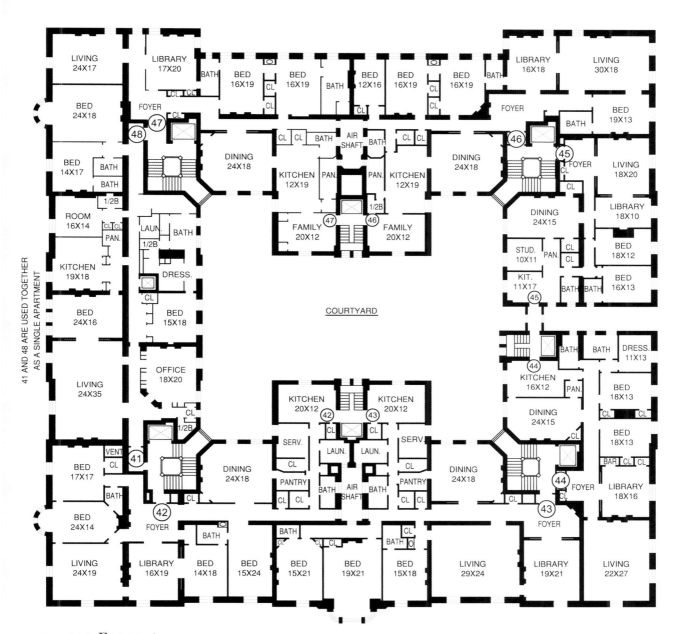

FIG. 102. FLOOR 4

FIG. 103. FLOOR 5

50 AND 51 ARE USED TOGETHER
AS A SINGLE APARTMENT

FIG. 104. FLOOR 6

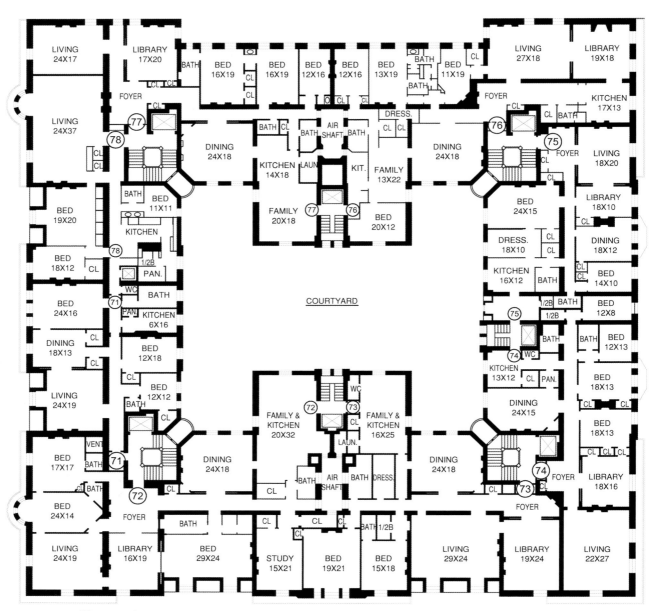

FIG. 105. FLOOR 7

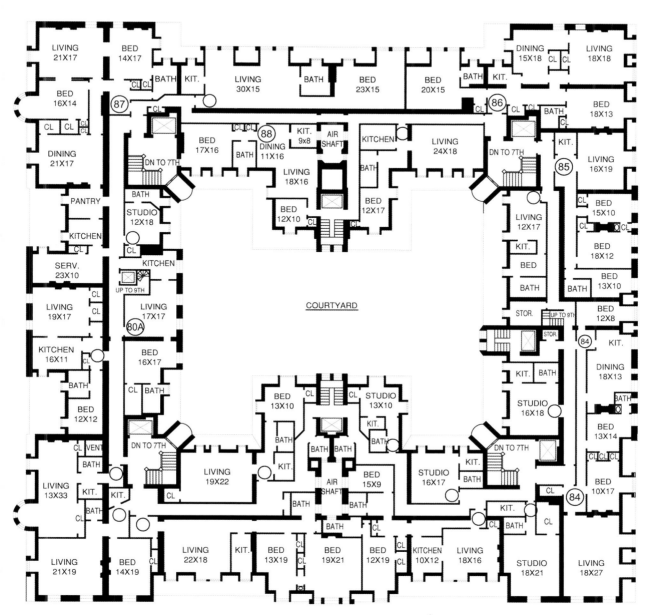

FIG. 106. FLOOR 8

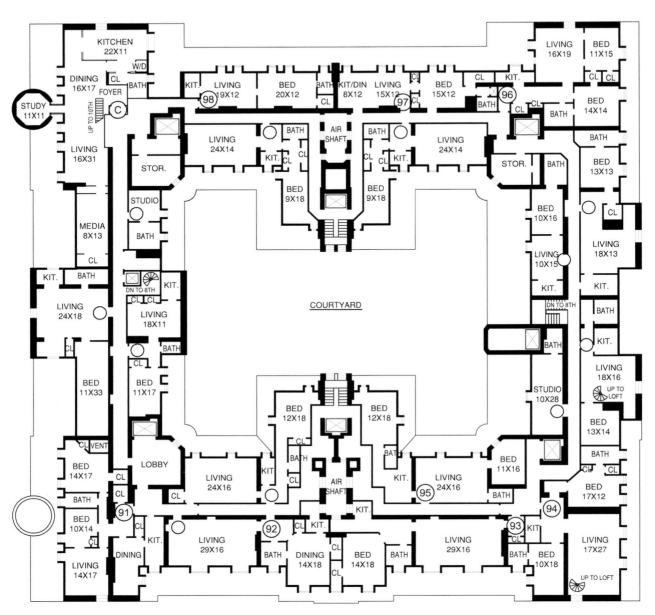

FIG. 107. FLOOR 9

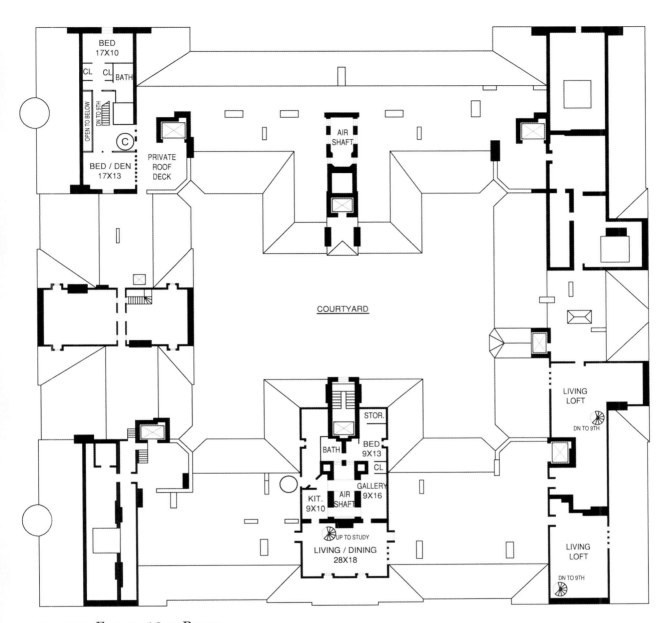

FIG. 108. FLOOR 10 & ROOF

FIG. 109. The Dakota's rooftop and courtyard complexity from the adjoining apartment house at 15 West 72 Street looking east to Central Park. *Columbus Ave.* magazine, October 1981

FIG. 110. The Dakota from the northeast with the 1930 Majestic Apartments at 115 Central Park West at the left. At the right is the corner of the 1906 Langham at 135 Central Park West. *Kenneth Grant*

FIG. 111. The north façade of the Dakota with the 1964 Mayfair Tower apartment house at 15 West 72 Street behind it. *Kenneth Grant*

FIG. 112. The south façade along 72nd Street with a piece of the unadorned plain brick western face of the building, and a corner of Mayfair Tower at the left. *Kenneth Grant*

FIG. 113. The central portion of the north façade, with the open slot onto which windows to subsidiary rooms face. Just beneath the second-floor arch are two of the aerial passageways connecting one line of kitchens to the service elevator and stair. *Kenneth Grant*

FIG. 114. The central portion of the plain-brick western front of the Dakota showing the slate-covered mansard roof with its multiplicity of dormer windows. At the right is a corner of the white-brick Mayfair Tower apartments. Looming up in the background is the north tower of the Majestic Apartments with its sculptural quarter-round Art Deco ornamental top. *Kenneth Grant*

FIG. 115. The entrance façade on 72nd Street. *Kenneth Grant*

FIG. 116. The arched and groin-vaulted carriage entrance, now accommodating a modern carriage. *Kenneth Grant*

FIG. 117. The entrance from the sidewalk showing the original railings, and the early but non-original cast iron urns and metal-clad sentry box now used by the doormen. *Kenneth Grant*

FIG. 118. One of the gas-fed wall-mounted lanterns that were added to the building when the original pedestal-mounted lighting stanchions were removed. *Kenneth Grant*

FIG. 119. A detail of the east façade above Central Park West at the third and fourth floors, with a vacant sculpture niche. *Andrew Alpern*

FIG. 120. One of two turrets atop the rounded oriel windows on the south façade of the building. *Kenneth Grant*

Fɪɢ. 121. The upper gable of the south façade of the Dakota, showing a perhaps-Dakota Indian and the date when construction of the building began, following excavation work and the laying of the massive foundation. *Kenneth Grant*

FIG. 122. The two-story oriel in the center of the east façade along Central Park West. *Kenneth Grant*

FIG. 123. The corresponding central window feature on the south façade along 72nd Street. *Kenneth Grant*

FIG. 124. Elegant copper- and iron-work detailing on the mansard at the top of the east façade. *Michael Garrett*

FIG. 125. A bit of fantasy near the top of the central oriel overlooking Central Park. *Michael Garrett*

FIGS. 126, 127, 128, & 129. There are four portrait roundels on the Dakota, two carved into the light tan stone over the high entrance arch on 72nd Street (bottom), and two at the more reddish and flatter arch over the central triple window on the Central Park West façade at the first floor (top). No documentation has been found that definitively identifies the man and woman over the entrance, and the man's profile bears no relationship to that of either Edward Clark or Henry Hardenbergh, the two most likely models. But it is strikingly close to the appearance of Isaac Merritt Singer, Clark's business partner. And the woman is similar to Isabella Boyer Singer, the last wife of Mr. Singer. After Singer died in 1875, Clark had assisted Mrs. Singer with her successful assertion of rights to the Singer estate as the legal widow. Commemorating these two people in the façade of his new building venture would be a reasonable move for Clark to make. Identifying the couple on the avenue side is not so rewarding. They are not the obviously-stylized portraits that can be found on many buildings of that period, but neither do they look like any obvious candidates from among the people involved with the project whose photographs have been identified. *Michael Garrett*

FIG. 130. The Dakota from within Central Park in the Summer of 1891 when the north half of the Hotel San Remo (just peeking out from behind the tree in the right foreground) had been completed but the south half of the building had not yet been begun. This view is unusual because it shows the north façade of the Dakota in addition to the east one. Almost hidden by the shrubbery is a man in a straw boater leaning on the rustic railing of the small low bridge over a cove of the lake. Constructed using branches of trees, the rustic style was used within Central Park at that time for benches, pergolas, shelters, and for fences and railings, as here.

# CHAPTER 9

# Early residents of the Dakota

LISTED BELOW are some of the early residents of the Dakota through 1890, gleaned from several different social directories, census records, voter lists, and other sources. We have attempted to omit servants and resident employees, but still these lists are subjective and not to be totally relied upon. The original records are often incomplete, inconsistent, difficult to read, open to interpretation, and sometimes completely wrong, so this list should be read with a good deal of skepticism, or as Dakota resident Mr. Rufus Hicks might have said, *cum grano salis*.

| YEAR FIRST RECORDED | NAME | OCCUPATION | PRIOR ADDRESS |
|---|---|---|---|
| 1886 | Mr. & Mrs. Robert E. Wescott | president, express co. | 361 West 46 Street |
| | Mr. & Mrs. William J. Brown | segars | 152 West 57 Street The Rembrandt |
| | Mr. & Mrs. Edgar Deale | broker | 64 West 22 Street |
| | Mr. & Mrs. Boye C. Boysen | broker | Brooklyn |
| | Mr. & Mrs. William F. Pippey died in place c.1930 | dry goods | 911 Seventh Avenue |
| | Mr. & Mrs. Emil Herold | merchant | Hoboken |
| | Mr. & Mrs. Lemuel E. Wells | coal | 48 East 79 Street |
| | Mr. & Mrs. Rufus Hicks | lawyer | 49 West 57 Street |
| | Mrs. Harriet M. Edey | widow of Albert, broker | 110 West 123 Street |
| | Mr. & Mrs. Dominique Verdenal | secretary | 228 West 44 Street |
| | Mr. & Mrs. Solon J. Vlasto | merchant | 72 West 92 Street |
| | Alfred, Walter, and Mrs. M. Mack | clothing | 325 West 58 Street |
| | Mrs. James Baremore | widow of James, diamonds | 295 West 57 Street |
| | Mr. & Mrs. T. Cave de Luce | | |
| | Mr. & Mrs. C. Francis Bates he born 1825 | trimmings | 3 East 22 Street |
| | Mr. Charles F. Bates | stenographer | |
| | Mr. Albert Griesbach | linens | |
| | Mr. & Mrs. John White | | |
| | Mr. & Mrs. Tarrant Putnam died in place c.1930 | lawyer | 117 East 72 Street |
| | Mrs. Charles Knoblauch | broker | 334 West 18 Street |
| | Mr. Maxwell D. Howell still in place 1933 | | |

| 1887 | Mr. & Mrs. Frederick G. Bourne | agent for Clark family | |
| | Mr. & Mrs. Edward D. Faulkner | upholstered goods | |
| | Mr. & Mrs. Edward H. Faulkner | upholstered goods | |
| | Mr. Harry W. Mack | | |
| | Mr. Walter Mack | | |
| | Mr. & Mrs. Adolph Obrig<br>died in place c.1930 | stock broker | he born 1845 |
| | Prof. & Mrs. John K. Rees | Columbia College | 15 East 79 Street |
| | Mr. and Mrs. Gustav Schirmer | music publisher | 32 West 53 Street |
| | Mr. Rudolph Schirmer | | |
| | Mr. & Mrs. Frank K. Sprague | | |
| | Mr. Julius H. von Sachs | broker | 137 West 23 Street |
| | Mr. & Mrs. William von Sachs | broker | 137 West 23 Street |
| | Mr. William von Sachs, Jr. | broker | 137 West 23 Street |
| | Mr. & Mrs. Erastus Tucker Tefft | dry goods | 715 Fifth Avenue |
| 1889 | Mr. & Mrs. Calvin H. Allen | vice president | Hotel Vendome |
| | Mr. & Mrs. Henry Budge | broker | 132 West 57 Street |
| | Mr. & Mrs. Alfred A. Cowles | vice president | 200 West 56 Street<br>The Van Corlear |
| | Mr. Edgar Deal | | |
| | Miss. Cornelia V. Deal<br>still in place 1933 | | |
| | Mr. & Mrs. Jacob S. Farley | broker | Plainfield, NJ |
| | Mr. & Mrs. Harvey Fisk | banker | |
| | Mr. & Mrs. Charles I. Hudson | broker | |
| | Mr. & Mrs. John H. Kemp | canned goods | 72 West 52 Street |
| | Mr. Robert Coleman Kemp | physician | |
| | Mr. & Mrs. John F. Miller | insurance | |
| | Mrs. Eliza Nye | | |
| | Mr. Edward Rothschild | | Hoboken |
| | Mr. & Mrs. Frank Griswold Tefft | dry goods | 715 Fifth Avenue |
| | Mr. Walter O. Whitcomb | beds | 222 West 23 Street<br>The Chelsea |
| | Mr. & Mrs. James H. Walsh | | |
| | Mr. & Mrs. George S. Weston | broker | 41 West 42 Street |
| | Mr. George H. Chatterton | | 168 East 64 Street |
| | Mr. A. Howard Hopping | importer | 356 West 61 Street |
| | Mr. Theodor D. Howell | merchant | 200 West 56 Street<br>The Van Corlear |
| | Mrs. Mary Saxton | | |
| | Mr. Frank D. Shaw | lawyer | 10 West 30 Street |
| | Mrs. Sallie Carr Shaw | | |
| 1890 | William H. Merrill<br>born 1855 | educator (at NYU?) | |

| | | |
|---|---|---|
| Merrill or Morris Stransky | | |
| C.R. and S.A. Hammerslough | clothing | |
| Julius Hammerslough | clothing | |
| Louis Hammerslough | clothing | Hotel Vendome |
| John A. Browning | founder, Browning School | |
| John E. Hasler | | |
| Chester and Augusta Billings <br> he born 1838 | | |
| Joseph H. Parsons | | |
| James W. Moore | physician | |
| Harmon I. Reees | | |
| Samuel and Lidia Barton | broker | |
| John and Florence White | | |
| George and Johanna Borgfeldt | merchant | 200 West 57 Street |
| William R. Smith | millinery | |
| James L. Livingston | insurance | |
| William C. Doscher | mirrors and frames | 263 West 11 Street |
| James and Carrie Calm | leather goods and novelties | 156 East 72 Street |
| Charles Benedict | | |
| Edwin Benten | | |
| George Breck | | |
| Albert and Rosa Gruseback | | |
| John Gunther | broker | |
| Henry Johns | asbestos, paints, roofing | |
| Isaiah and Silvia Josephi | clothing | |
| Harry Leonard | | |
| Thomas Lynch | | |
| Henry McCoun | merchant | |
| David McKelvy | | |
| Francis Putnam | | |
| William St. John | | |
| Eugene Sampson | | |
| Clara Hitchcock | merchant | |
| E. Eppel Wells | merchant | |
| Edward Thaw | merchant | |
| Jan Uhl | merchant | |
| Grover Schesteman | merchant | |
| Frederick Coykendall | corporate secretary, Columbia University | |
| Alfred Cammeyer | merchant | |
| Emil Long | | |
| Milissa Atterbury | | |
| Charles Fisher | piano maker | |
| George Schemerhoz | retired lawyer | |
| Albert Hiltoyz | retired merchant | |

| | |
|---|---|
| William Bippeer | merchant |
| Jonathan Browning | |
| Annie H. Howell | |
| Emma Harper | |
| Edgar Farkwar | merchant |
| John Selines | |
| Douglas Alexander | lawyer |
| James H. DeForrest | |
| Frederick Moore | |
| William E. Mees | astronomy professor |
| Herzog Bridge | |
| James Bridge | |
| Mari Faye | |
| Charles Fisher | |
| W. Gravis | |
| G. B. Harvey | |
| E, Matthiessen | |
| George Nullard | |
| Robert and Frances Schoppell | |
| George and Elizabeth Chattenden | |
| William and Olivia Brown | |

As noted above, the music publisher Mr. Gustav Schirmer lived at the Dakota. When Peter Illyich Tchaikovsky was in New York in 1891 as part of his only concert tour in North America, Mr. and Mrs. Schirmer gave a dinner party in his honor. Writing about the experience in a letter to a friend, Tchaikovsky said,

> De Sachs came to fetch me at twelve o'clock. We walked into the park. Then we went up by the lift to the fourth floor of an immense house where Schirmer lives. Besides myself and Sachs, there were at table the conductor Seidl, a Wagnerian and well known in this country, his wife, the pianist Adele Aus-der-Ohe, who is going to play at my concert, her sister, and the Schirmer family. Seidl told me that my Maid of Orleans would be produced next season. I had to be at rehearsal by four o'clock. De Sachs accompanied me to the Music Hall in the Schirmers' carriage. it was lit up and in order for the first time to-day. I sat in Carnegie's box, while an oratorio, The Shulamite, by the elder Dameosch, was being rehearsed. Before my turn came they sung a wearisome cantata by Schultz, The Seven Words. My choruses went very well. After it was over. I accompanied Sachs very unwillingly to the Schirmers', as he had made me promise to come back. We found a number of people there who had come merely to see me. Schirmer took us on the roof of his house. This huge, nine-storied house has a roof so arranged that one can take quite a delightful walk on it and enjoy a splendid view from all sides. The sunset was indescribably beautiful. When we went downstairs we found only a few intimate friends left, with whom I enjoyed myself most unexpectedly. Aus-der-Ohe played beautifully. Among other things, we played my Concerto together. We sat down to supper at nine o'clock. About 10:30 we, that is Sachs, Aus-der-Ohe, her sister, and myself, were presented with the most splendid roses, conveyed downstairs in the lift and sent home in the Schirmers' carriage. One must do justice to American hospitality; there is nothing like it—except, perhaps, in our own country.

# CHAPTER 10

# The aftermath of the Dakota

T HE CONSTRUCTION of the Dakota took four years, and during that time, considerable additional building activity was underway in the immediate vicinity and farther afield on the Upper West Side. It is a reasonable assumption that at least a portion of that investment would not have been made were it not for the expected completion of an instant landmark. Of course, the extension of the Ninth Avenue elevated railway in 1879 to service the area was also a strong impetus for developers and other investors to loosen their purse strings and take advantage of the area's growth potential. The five years immediately following the completion of the Dakota saw an unprecedented level of building activity. *The New York Sun* described the result in an article it published on Saturday, 23 March 1889.

### THE WONDERFUL WEST SIDE
### ITS CHANGE IS A MARVEL TO THOSE WHO KNEW IT IN ITS DESOLATION.

A Splendid New City Built Up Where Five Years Ago There Were Only Rocks, Swamps, Goats and Shanties • Substantial Tenements, Comfortable Apartments, and Handsome Private Residences for the People there Wasn't Room for in the Overcrowded East Side • The Elevated Railroad Has Done Much, But Additional Facilities for Rapid Transit Would Work New Wonders • Going To Keep Right On Growing And Improving The Real Estate Men Say

I t is a truism to say that the growth of the west side of this city has been and is simply marvelous. Within the last five years a territory which was only known to New Yorkers as being but little better than a wilderness of rocks and goats and swamps and shanties, which inspired the most desolate feelings in the beholder, has, metaphorically, blossomed like the rose and become the scene of a great addition to the city's life. The rocks have vanished, the swamps have become solid earth, and the goats are all dead. The homes of modern New York are up there now. Thousands of beautiful and substantial structures stand in place of the rickety shanties. The city west of Central Park, between Fifty-ninth and Ninety-sixth streets has really become a new city, as unlike the rest of New York almost as the rest of New York is unlike Boston or Philadelphia. So quickly has this been accomplished that many people cannot yet believe that it is a fact. As they have gone up town on the Ninth avenue elevated road they have seen the busy little steam drills puffing away with ceaseless vigor at the big masses of rock all around; but there seemed so much of the rock and so little of the steam drill that the latter, after all, was only apt to provoke a smile. It seemed as though to get the rock out of the way would be the work of a life-time. But the rock is nearly all gone – at least between the streets referred to – and there are houses of brick and stone, flats, tenements, apartment houses, and private residences is their place.

The SUN presents to its readers this morning a graphic illustration of the progress made in building on the west side of the city during the last five years. The diagram speaks for itself better than any words or description can speak for it. In comparison with the buildings erected since 1884 those erected before that time seem almost insignificant in number. They seem to hang feebly to a corner or to be built at haphazard in the middle of a block. Even real estate men and others familiar with the great strides made in building in the last few years will probably be surprised at this exhibit of the number of houses built in this time. Before 1884 there were hardly any substantial houses at all between Eighth Avenue and the North River, and between Seventy-fourth and Ninety-sixth streets. There was a little cluster of brownstone fronts in Ninety-third Street, between Eighth and Ninth avenues. These, the most ambitious houses in the neighborhood, were erected by Boss Tweed in the vain attempt to start building in that portion of the city. Today they are about the worse looking building up there. Between Seventy-fourth and Ninety-sixth streets there were few houses on the side streets. There were no houses on Eleventh avenue, but two or three houses on Eighth and Ninth avenues, and but few more on Tenth avenue. While the building now is around Ninth Avenue as a centre, before 1884 Tenth Avenue seemed likely to become the great popular thoroughfare. The two triangular pieces of land between Seventieth and Sixty-sixth streets, and between Seventy-third and Seventy-fifth streets formed by the two intersections of Tenth Avenue and the Boulevard, were quite covered with houses. Houses were at the street corners for a good distance up the broad avenue. But there was nothing like solid blocks of flats and apartments and tenements and private residences. The building was all desultory and scattered. The great Dakota flats erected years before on Eighth avenue, between Seventy-Second and Seventy-third streets, loomed up magnificently, as it does still, but it did not draw near it any structures of a like nature, or apparently stimulate building of any kind in the least. It was the pioneer building in the region, but its good work was years in bearing fruit.

## CAUSES THAT LED TO THE BUILDING UP OF THE WEST SIDE.

The cause which diverted building from Tenth to Ninth avenue was also the cause of the surprising activity in building on the west side generally—the building of the Ninth Avenue elevated road. With the completion of the road through Ninth Avenue people began to travel over it, often for amusement, from the Battery to 155th street. Many people went over the road that had never been north of Central Park before. They were crowded, many of them, in close, dingy houses on the east side.

The universal cry went up: "Why cannot we have better homes? Homes more roomy, better lighted, better ventilated, in this new region?"

There were two reasons why they could not easily. The land on the west side, most of it was owned by speculators, who hold on to their property like grim death, and refused to sell it to anybody. The building of the elevated road forced some of this land out of the hands of these people, and, in a way, made subsequent purchases more easy. But they were still difficult. Besides, the rocky and in some places the swampy condition of the ground made a great many people hesitate about buying real estate there for building purposes. There were engineers who declared that some of the rock was practically irremovable. There were still more engineers who affirmed that if the rock was removed it could only be at enormous cost. The same difficulties were gravely alleged in regard to filling in the low, marshy lots. But all these soon became as naught in the face of the tremendous pressure of the population in the lower part of the city. People crowded each other and declared that they must have elbow room. Homes on the east side became scarce. There was a demand on the part of people, especially young people, for a chance to secure modern homes at moderate prices, which could be purchased on the installment plan. So that those buying might get the benefit of their own savings.

These were the primal causes, undoubtedly, of the building up on the west wide. But, by themselves, they would not have been apt to take a clear and effective form. It needed some head, some directing agency. In a little while, after the presence of the need made itself felt in the community, there came to its aid the most practical and efficient helper possible, a vast quantity of unemployed capital in the hands of the *great* banking and business firms. Such corporations as the Equitable and Mutual Life Insurance Companies eagerly availed themselves of this need and anxiety of the people of the city for homes upon the west side. Private capital, too, was wide-awake. It would be Interesting to know just how much money in the early part of 1884 was placed in the hands of real estate agents for the purchase and improvement of land on the west side. The building upon the land since that time, as shown by the illustration, affords, in some degree, at least, a basis for a calculation. When it is remembered that the cost of thousands of new and elegant structures was probably, after all, not greater than the cost of buying and improving the land on which they stood, some idea of the money invested in the west side may be obtained. Real estate brokers were themselves eagerly alive to the situation. They borrowed largely from the big capitalists, besides using all their own available money. In many instances the banks and others investing money employed agents of their own.

## WHO WERE FIRST IN THE FIELD

Real estate men generally give the credit of the first building on the west side to the Clark estate, or, in reality, the money of the Singer Sewing Machine Company. Mr. Clark was not discouraged by the failure of the Dakota flats to bring about an increase of building near it. In the early part of 1880 he told his friends that the time had come to build, and build he did. He put up in quick succession house after house in Seventy-second and Seventy-third streets. The news-papers praised Mr. Clark for his courage, and printed articles eulogistic of the west side. Then Builders Merritt and Luyster put up beautiful structures in Seventy-Sixth streets and West End Avenue.

People were no longer timid. Owners of property stopped looking at each other and saying:

"Well, you go on and build, and then I will."

The Equitable Insurance Company invested largely in Harlem and the Mutual Life people in the middle section of the west side. Money went around in the real estate offices at 4 percent, and not a little was lent at $3\frac{1}{2}$ percent, and even at $3\frac{1}{4}$ percent. The general impression seemed to be among moneyed men that investments on the west side were extremely safe, even if the returns were small at first.

Among the real estate men who were quick to see the possibilities and future of the new territory, and who did not have to think twice before investing in property there and advising their customers to invest, were P. H. McManus. Ninth avenue and 135th street: Folsom Brothers, 58 East Thirteenth street: Gnerineau & Drake, 11 Bible House: Wilmot & Jarvis, 1,808 Third avenue; J. Edgar Leaycraft. 1544 Broadway; John R. Foley, 153 Broadway; Just Brothers, 709 Broadway: Anthony Arent, Ninth avenue and Eighty–third street; Joseph Levy & Son, 373 Eighth avenue: Morris B. Baer, 72 West Thirty-fourth Street; Brodi & Betty, 1,216 Third avenue; L. H. da Cunha, Broadway and Forty second street; C. F. Street, 359 West Fifty-ninth street; J. Romaine Brown, 59 West Thirty-third street; Thomas A. Vyse, 66 Liberty street; Potter & Brothers. Ninth avenue and Eighty-second street; Stevens, Ninth avenue and Ninety-third street; F. G. Davis, Ninth avenue, near Ninety-third street, and John H. Blake, 265 Broadway, whose success in developing Brentwood, Long Island, is fresh in the minds of the public. When these men took hold of things people began to come in with a rush, and there was no longer any hesitation.

## CHARACTER AND DISTRIBUTION OF THE NEW BUILDINGS.

Building lingered for a while in the neighborhood of Seventy-second Street, where it started, and was for a time confined to residence houses. Then by one of those freaks familiar to people in the real estate business it leaped up to Ninety-third Street, and the building of flats and tenement houses began. Then it came back down town again to Sixty-third and adjacent streets. Since then building has spread in all directions on the west side. Flats, tenement houses and residences have gone up like magic everywhere. An examination of the diagram shows that the Ninth avenue elevated railroad has been the center of attraction. At first sight it might seem hard to classify the section in regard to the character of the buildings erected, but close inspection shows that the building has progressed steadily and surely within certain very plainly marked lines of development.

Ninth Avenue is the home of tenements, of five and six and even more stories. On the ground floor of these tenements are rooms for stores and other business establishments. People along here say that they want a horse car line badly for local traffic. It is true that the elevated road is there, and that there are surface railroads on all the other avenues. But the Ninth avenue people say that they feel intensely the need of a horse-car line, and that a horse-car line they must have. Of course, tenements have been erected in all parts of the district, but there are more of them around Ninth Avenue than there are anywhere else. The part of each tenement occupied by a family has, as a rule, from four to six rooms, and rents at all the way from $12 to $35 a month. It is hardly fair to say that some of the more costly tenements are not apartment houses. They have carpeted hallways, bathrooms and all the conveniences found in the high-class apartment structure. They are good enough for anybody to live in. A constant improvement is apparent in the new buildings going up, said Architect and Builder Charles Buek of 187 Ninth avenue to a Sun reporter:

"The first buildings erected here in the neighborhood of Seventy-second street are not such as builders would put up now. They are just as strong, of course, but they are not so elegant. Five years ago if we had put up such tenements and apartments as we are now erecting people would have said we were crazy. But now they are satisfied with the buildings erected then. The reason is, of course, that property down here has improved enormously in value since the times of the old buildings, and our new buildings must show a commensurate improvement. The demand is constantly for more elaborate buildings. I think all the people who came here are entirely satisfied. People who came there first did so, in great measure, because they were crowded out of the east side. Now they come here because they like and choose the west side. Rents are going up all the time."

The stores beneath the Ninth avenue dwellings rent at $100 to $500 a month.

Eighth Avenue seems as yet to be little built up. Fronting on Central Park, as it does, it will undoubtedly be devoted in future to apartment houses of the first class, such as the Dakota flats, renting for high prices. The retarding of the growth here is ascribed by real estate men to various causes, but the fact seems to be that the land is held for speculative purposes, or rather by people who refuse to sell it, in the hope of a large future rise in value. The holdings of estates here are very large. As yet there has been no severe pressure upon the owners for a sale of their property for building purposes. Most of the people, so far, who have gone up on the west side to live are people of moderate means, who have not demanded the magnificent apartment houses or residences such as Eighth avenue can only be devoted to.

Along Tenth avenue, and to a great extent on corner lots wherever they may be, have been erected what the real estate men known as "good, fair apartment houses." These are, in reality, such elegant structures as the "Ormonde" at Eighty-sixth street and Ninth avenue, built and owned by Prague & Power, the real estate agents who have done so much for Eighty-sixth street and its neighborhood. The tendency seems to be not to go up town in the building of these flats. They stay down below Ninety-sixth Street, though the Shenandoah flats at 135th street and Ninth Avenue, owned by P. H. McManus, the big real estate man of that section, are a notable exception. They rent at $30 to $80 a month. Property in this section is held at first-rate values, and the building is all of a kind that is meant to stay. It is hardly necessary to say that the houses are designed with the utmost care to provide every comfort and luxury. The flats have from six to ten rooms on an average. It is not the fashion longer to give them names.

The cross streets between Fifty-ninth and Ninety-sixth streets are turned over to the residences, through on the corners of these streets have been built some of the more elegant of the flats. The builders of the majority of these houses have put them up with the idea of selling them and they do sell them at anywhere from $35,000 to $60,000. These houses rent at from $1,200 to $2,500 a year apiece. Here, as nowhere else, is the modern character of the building on the west side seen. Everything about the houses is new and fresh. It is unlike anything in any part of the city. It seems truly the home of the fashionable New Yorker of the future. Nothing can be more picturesque than one of these streets, with its new and varied styles of architecture, its bay and octagonal windows in pretty colored stone, looking out on broad freestone pavements. Often polished ash and oaken handrails lead down the front steps to the sidewalk. The houses, most of them, are built of Jersey and Philadelphia pressed brick. But it is in the facings that the chief beauty and picturesqueness appear. The favorite ones are, besides the popular brown stone, the white limestone and granite, the light brown Belleville stone, the red Lake Superior, and the blue Wyoming. They are carved and fretted into all sorts of pretty designs. The interior decorations of these houses are elaborate. They have permanent fireplace and sideboard fixtures. They are fitted up on the different floors in ash and oak, cherry and walnut, and have hardwood floors. The drawing room floors in many of them are in mosaic. There is no getting around the fact that Seventy-second and Eighty-sixth streets, with Eighty-first and eighty-fourth streets are looked upon just now as the particularly handsome streets in this part of the city.

But it is the West End Avenue and Riverside drives that are going to be the cream and pride of this section. The residences going up there are simply palaces. People who live there are confident that theirs is the future Fifth Avenue of the city. A mere glance at these broad, finely paved avenues and the high ground on which they are located shows the reason for this belief. At present the houses in West End Avenue are mostly between Seventieth and Seventy-sixth streets, but new ones are going up constantly. Property along Riverside drive is still held for speculative purposes, and building there is not progressing rapidly. There are few buildings along the Boulevard, too, from Seventy-sixth Street up.

### A PERMANENT AND HEALTHY GROWTH.

Nearly all real estate men agree that this wonderful development of the west side, despite its rapidity, has been steady and natural, and entirely called for by the situation. The growth had not been fictitious. There has been an absurdly small number of business failures in proportion to the almost fabulous amount of money involved. The buildings have been erected in a sound and careful manner. They are preeminently modern, they have been built in accordance with new and severe building and sanitary laws, and every effort has been made to secure safety, roominess, light, and ventilation. Their location is preeminently healthful, standing as it does high above Murray Hill, and almost on a level with the Palisades on the Jersey side of the Hudson. In all this growth there has been no retrograde movement. There have been lulls at times, but nothing of a downfall. The best judgment of experts is that property between Fifty-ninth and Ninety-sixth streets and between Central Park and the North River has increased in value 50 percent, since 1884, and this puts the story in a nutshell. The Ninth avenue elevated railroad is contemplating, and has, in fact, about decided to erect four new stations in this district. This will give another boom to west side property. There are stations now at Fifty-ninth, Seventy-second, Eighty-first. Ninety-third, and 104th streets. The new stations will be at Sixty-sixth, Seventy-sixth, Eighty-sixth, and Ninety-eighth streets.

Forty-three years later, a critique of the Dakota appeared in The Sky Line column of *The New Yorker* magazine for 19 March 1932.

### A SURVIVOR OF THE BROWN DECADES

The new exercises in period modernism along Central Park West cause one's eyes to linger with extra pleasure on the Dakota Apartments, one of the few survivors of the spacious manners of the Brown Decades. In the course of fifty years or so, the Dakota has really worn very well: a solid, commodious, respectable building. I daresay its high ceilings take a pretty heavy toll in housekeeping and domestic service—the hangings are almost twice as long and the moldings twice as high as in the ordinary apartments of today—but will our half-baked "modern" apartment houses that are now springing up along the Park look half as real and convincing fifty years from now?

I will answer that question. Absolutely not! The modernism of these buildings is merely a thin veneer: banked corner windows that light long narrow rooms; occasional terraces fitfully disposed about the upper parts of the structure; massive brick enclosures of water tanks. Even the relatively plain façades do not authenticate these structures. The most helpful feature about a great many of the new apartment houses is the increasing breadth of the windows. The fear of sunlight and air, which we quaintly think confined to the French, is beginning to disappear among the well-to-do, who have so often been content with dark, back-to-back houses and apartments which differed only in price, space, and internal cleanliness from our worst slums. But these apartments are far from being solid and useful examples of modern architecture, and they do not give a hint of what a good architect could do were he able to work on land of reasonable price and on plots large enough to permit effective planning. In all essentials the Dakota is as close to organic architecture as its most up-to-date neighbor: that is, they are both about fifty years away from the real thing.

The following year, on 21 November 1933, the *New York Times* reported on a meeting of the Central Park West Association that was held in the Dining Room of the Dakota.

### BUS SEEKERS TALK OF HORSE-CAR DAYS

George P. Douglass, who remembers when Central Park West was "tickled to death" with its new horse-cars, attended a luncheon yesterday at which directors of the Central Park West Association expressed the hope of soon being able to away with "the old-fashioned electric trolley."

Speakers described the surface cars as "noisy, uncomfortable and unsightly," and every one present agreed that they would soon be supplanted by the bus. The directors also adopted a resolution felicitating Mr. Douglass on the completion of thirty-six years as manager of the Dakota Apartments, at Central Park West and Seventy-second Street, in which the luncheon was held.

The Dakota is the oldest apartment building on the west side of the park, having only two small brownstone contemporaries in the block. These, sandwiched between towering hotels, do not count, as they were not apartments originally but private homes. The rest were shanties, and the Dakota's record is clear all the way down to Fifth-sixth Street and Seventh Avenue, where another, less impressive, apartment house stood when the Dakota was built in 1881.

After the association had agreed to take a poll of the neighborhood as to quality of bus service and rate of fare desired, and to present its findings to the incoming Board of Estimate, Mr. Douglass exhibited old engravings and photographs of the Dakota and yellowed newspapers in which its splendors were described at length.

THE NEW YORK TIMES of Oct. 22, 1884, the year when the first tenants moved in, devoted more than a column to the refinements lavished upon the building by the architect, H. J. Hardenbergh, who also designed the old Waldorf and the Plaza. "On the Seventy-third Street side there is a handsome doorway, and on the Seventy-second Street front a fine arched carriage entrance, with groined roof and elegant stone carving. Both entrances lead into the inner court, from which four separate passages afford access to the interior of the building.."

The description serves as well today as it did in 1884, for nothing has been changed. The surroundings, on the other hand, have been materially altered. Where the Majestic now stands was formerly a group of flimsy shacks surrounded by truck gardens and enclosures for live stock.

The Dakota has always been a part of the Edwin Severin Clark estate, and Stephen

Carlton Clark, who recently inherited it, has announced that it will continue to be run along the same lines as formerly. Two of its original tenants, both in their eighties, still retain apartments there; four others have died there in the last three years.

The basement of the Dakota is full of large intricate machinery, suggesting the engine-room of an ocean liner. There is a huge pump to take care of the hydraulic elevators and beneath the old-fashioned landscaped park on the west side of the building are three electric dynamos , and boilers that at one time furnished heat to virtually the entire block.

There are large storage compartments in which a reserve of 1,000 tons of coal is always kept, "just in case of emergency," and a complete laundry. "We have to get water, groceries and coal outside; otherwise we are practically an independent commonwealth here," said Mr. Douglass proudly.

The Dakota is only nine stories high, but owing to its lofty ceilings can look down upon modern fifteen-story buildings.

Russell B. Corey, president of the association, presided at the luncheon. The principal speaker was Harold J. Treanor, counsel for the Real Estate Board of New York, who discussed regulations of the new Alcoholic Beverage Control Board. The organization also paid tribute to the memory of the late Charles J. Quinian, a former vice president.

The edition of the *Herald-Tribune* of the same date, 21 November 1933, also reported on the same luncheon.

### DAKOTA, HOTEL 50 YRS., LOOKS FORWARD TO 100

Fifteen members of a West Side real estate fraternity, some of whom remember when squatters' goats rambled the fields of Seventy-second Street and horsecars jangled up and down Central Park West, arose from their seats at a cluttered luncheon table well after noon yesterday and solemnly extended felicitations to an apartment house. They had lunched in the private dining room of the Dakota, aristocrat of the West Side, and they had just been informed that having rounded out a half-century as a nine-story structure, the Dakota stood an excellent chance of passing another fifty years without material change in its appearance, character or traditional demeanor of aloofness.

Tenants of the spacious floors above the dining room, two of whom have lived nowhere else since the Dakota was opened for public inspection in 1883, had learned the day before that Stephen Carlton Clark, brother of Edward Severin Clark, the original owner, who died two months ago, had not the remotest intention of tearing down the Dakota, remodeling it or selling its protective square of lawn. George P. Douglass, the manager who has been associated with the building for thirty-six years had informed them that there was no longer any need to worry. "Mr. Stephen," he had announced to each tenant, "will entertain none of the offers which have caused us consternation in past weeks. He has so informed me in person."

Yesterday, Mr. Douglass gravely made the same announcement to the members of the Central Park and Columbus Avenue Association meeting at the Dakota, as is their custom. A resolution was unanimously adopted felicitating the Dakota itself and tendering congratulations to its manager and to the new owner. While brief, lightly sentimental addresses were delivered, a log fire flickered quietly in the recesses of the rambling lobby, bequeathing a crimson glow to the polished brass of the original doorknobs and to the massive doors and panels of rich quartered oak. The thick walls of the Dakota, hand-built by stone masons of another age, preserved for the lunchers a friendly warmth and silenced the sounds of traffic on the streets outside.

The Dakota had weathered other, earlier storms, during which there had been loose talk of demolition, but it had never before been subjected to the crisis occasioned by a change of ownership. Edward Severin Clark was one of the heirs to the fortune founded on the Singer Sewing Machine Company. Having inherited the site from his grandfather, he reared the Dakota from a cornerstone laid in 1880; and he had been the sole owner until he died in September. Besides maintaining its air of outward austerity and inward hospitality, the building appeared to take on an appearance of something close to smugness yesterday.

Its walls paraded as usual from Seventy-second to Seventy-third, facing the wide acres of Central Park. An arm of lawn, worth $350,000 today, and more in boom times, extended for half a city block toward the west, adequately preventing upstart structures from jostling the Dakota or even approaching close enough to place it in shadow. Huddled about were a handful of newcomers, ogling at the rare bit of vacant space with thousands of close-set windows: but none of these was nearer than the breadth of a full-sized thoroughfare. With its fastidious gables, its stout bay windows and its built-in driveway fashioned for coaches-and-four, the Dakota stood firmly on its unimpeachable foundation – somewhat shorter than its neighbors, but immeasurably more impressive.

.   .   .

Mr. Douglass . . . expressed something of what he felt as he led reporters around the rambling old building and talked about its history. He produced some old photographs taken from the roof of the Dakota, showing a strange expanse of squatters shacks in all directions, and horsecars meandering up the unpaved road that is now Central Park West.

"The Dakota," he said, "was called 'Clark's Folly' in the eighties, you know. Probably it was called 'Dakota' because it was so far west, and so far north."

FIG. 131. An oil painting on panel of a detail of the 72nd Street entrance to the Dakota by Richard Britell

# CHAPTER 11

# The Clark family
# after the Dakota

EDWARD CLARK had three sons and a daughter. In 1836, Ambrose Jordan Clark was born, named after his grandfather who was also his father's law partner. In 1838, Edward Lorraine Clark was born, and then in 1841 their sister Julia came into the world, only to leave it two months later. Finally, in 1844 Alfred Corning Clark was born, the only child of Edward and Caroline Clark to survive his father.

He in turn eventually had four sons of his own, the only grandchildren of Edward Clark. The three generations of the Clark family have had an indelible impact on the architecture of New York City. Edward Clark started it off with the Van Corlear apartment house, then built the Ontiora and Wyoming apartment houses plus two other smaller apartment houses and 51 individual rowhouses in two long groupings, ending with the Dakota, which wasn't completed until two years after his death.

Edward Clark's youngest child became his heir when the elder Clark died in 1882, taking over the operation of his real estate empire. Even before the Dakota was finished, in 1883 Alfred Corning Clark hired architect Charles W. Romeyn (1854-1942) for what became known as the Dakota Stables, taking up the southerly blockfront of 75th Street between Amsterdam Avenue and Broadway (fig. 132).

Romeyn designed a robust, picturesque, Romanesque-style structure of brick and brownstone, three stories high, the third expressed as a long mansard. The ground floor served as an assembly area, and there were 145 stalls for horses on the second floor. The stated cost of construction was $60,000, about $400 per horse. For comparison, the Dakota's cost was often said to be $2 million; if there were 250 residents among its 60-odd apartments, that would be about $8,000 per person. In 1883, the *Real Estate Record & Guide* announced that the stables would be "in connection with the Dakota," but neither the *New York Sun* nor the *New York Times* nor a wide variety of magazines carried any article or any advertisement designed to attract customers. There is no evidence that the stables were built specifically for Dakota residents. Boarding and livery stables were in short supply on the newly developed West Side. Like other big stables it served as a sort of club and office for coachmen and grooms; in 1895 *The Times* carried a position-wanted ad for a coachman named P. Jones, who described himself as a "young colored man" who was "generally useful; very neat," and asked for replies care of the Dakota Stables. The *New York Sun* reported variously that the aging structure had been sold by the Clarks (1902); would be replaced by a 14-story garage (1905); and was to make way for an apartment building (1906). But in 1910 it was altered to accommodate automobiles, and the Dakota name was taken up by a different stable, on Amsterdam and 77th Street, while the original Dakota Stables was known for a time as Dakota Auto Repair. A

Fig. 132. The Dakota Stables on West 75th Street between Amsterdam Avenue and Broadway, which were not part of Edward Clark's Dakota project but were built following Clark's death by Alfred Corning Clark, the elder Clark's only surviving son and heir.

1916 map shows a one-story structure on the site; the Hotel Beacon was built there in the 1920s, since converted to apartments. Clark also built a modest row of ten houses on the north side of West 85th Street between Central Park West and Columbus Avenue.

What sort of man was Alfred Corning Clark, and what architectural influence did he have? When his father died in 1882, he was 38 years old, had been married for 13 years and had four sons. The family lived in proper upper-class comfort at 7 West 22 Street, a conventional rowhouse that Edward Clark had owned (fig. 133). This would have been expected of a man who had just inherited from his father an estate worth about $50 million, primarily in the stock of the Singer Sewing Machine Company. His sons had inherited their grandfather's real estate empire, with three of the boys each gaining possession of an entire Manhattan city block 200 feet by 800 feet on the Upper West Side, and the fourth son an equivalent property in Midtown. While Alfred Clark may have appeared to have been conventional, he was unconventionally rich, and he was quite unconventional in other ways, which ultimately led to additional important construction projects in Manhattan.

Alfred Corning Clark evidenced an exceptional sensitivity and generosity that attracted him to creatively artistic people. He also had a personality that was attracted to particularly handsome young men. He established one of them – a Norwegian tenor – in an apartment in a pair of converted rowhouses at 64 West 22 Street, and spent much time there and with the man's family in Norway. Another, whom he met in Paris following the death of his Norwegian lover, was the American sculptor George Grey Barnard. This strikingly handsome, accomplished young man became Clark's "kept boy" in Paris and created sculptures for Clark. Eventually, Barnard married, moved to New York, and with financial assistance from Clark established a collection of medieval sculptural fragments, and pieces of ancient buildings. Barnard's mini-museum later became the basis for the Cloisters Museum in northern Manhattan, which opened originally in Barnard's studio.

Alfred Clark's love for music and his penchant for young men combined in his long involvement with the Mendelssohn Glee Club, an all-male singing society. In 1892, he built Mendelssohn

Hall as their club house at 119 West 40 Street, a building as designed by Robert H. Robertson that included an auditorium accommodating 1100 seats, a library, and apartments for bachelors. It may have been at the Mendelssohn Glee Club that Clark first met Frederick Gilbert Bourne, or possibly at the Mercantile Library where Bourne worked as a clerk, but regardless of the venue the meeting and subsequent relationship resulted in Alfred introducing Bourne to his father, who hired him as construction manager at the beginning of the Dakota project. Bourne demonstrated his abilities there, as Alfred leaned on him heavily after his father died. The overseeing of the Singer Sewing Machine Company was not an activity in which Alfred took any great interest, and in 1889 Alfred appointed Bourne its president. In that position, Bourne had a major impact on architecture and the development of the skyscraper.

In 1896, Bourne hired the talented but famously cranky architect Ernest Flagg to design a new Singer headquarters in New York at the northwest corner of Broadway and Liberty Street. Although skyscrapers were beginning to rise on steel frames, Flagg proclaimed himself against tall buildings and designed a Beaux-Arts-style bearing-wall structure.

A few years later Bourne had Flagg design what is called the "Little Singer Building" on Broadway near Prince Street (fig. 134). This was clearly a more ingenious design, integrating the need for well-lighted areas in an industrial building with a sophisticated mix of frankly exposed structural terra-cotta (until then used only as ornament), exposed steel, and ironwork of structural logic but great elegance that invoked the work of the French architect Viollet le Duc with floor-to-ceiling glass used as a design element. "The Rational Skyscraper" one article called it, even admiring its unusual color scheme.

Flagg had occasion to revise his views on the skyscraper with his next commission from Bourne. In 1902 he began the design of what would soon be the tallest building in the world, the

FIG. 133. The original Clark family home at 7 West 22 Street is to the left of this identical house.

FIG. 134. The "Little Singer Building" of 1902-1904 on Broadway near Prince Street by Ernest Flagg.

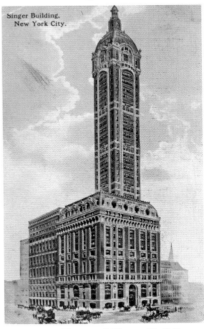

FIG. 135. The 1896 Singer Building with its 1908 tower Addition at its back corner.

FIG. 136. After Alfred Corning Clark died, his widow Elizabeth Clark built this mansion on Riverside Drive at 89th Street. This is how it appeared in 1905 when she lived there as the wife of Bishop Henry Potter.

47-story steel-framed Singer Tower at Broadway and Liberty Street (fig. 135), incorporating the 1896 bearing-wall building he had designed six years earlier. Flagg changed his opinion about steel frame construction but not about the menace of skyscrapers, deciding that such towers should rise from only 25 percent of the lot.

Indeed, it did rise, 612 feet, with a bulbous top that imitated a Singer factory in Scotland but otherwise sang out "Paris" like a can-can dancer at the Moulin Rouge. But other developers caught the skyscraper wave, and soon the Singer Tower was hemmed in by the City Investing Building – whose owner decided he preferred 100-percent lot coverage – and Flagg campaigned for the first height limits on skyscraper construction, culminating in the 1916 zoning resolution.

The Clark proclivity for building revived after Alfred Corning Clark's death on 8 April 1896, when his widow, Elizabeth, moved from the Clark family brownstone on West 22nd Street and commissioned Flagg to build an expansive French-style house on the Upper West Side overlook-

FIG. 137. The Clark Model Tenements on West 69th Street.

ing the Hudson River (fig. 136). Many forecast Riverside Drive as the "new Fifth Avenue" because of the wide plots and river views, and Elizabeth chose a sweeping, curving block-front between 89th and 90th Streets. Here Flagg designed his most sumptuous city residence in incandescent red brick and white marble, daringly angled away from the grid and toward the western view over the Hudson River. Although its near-cubic form gave it a Georgian air, the rich, robust French detailing – with lots of glass and surrounded by gardens and a high iron fence – gave the Clark mansion a breathlessly continental look. Flagg was particularly inventive in lining up a one-story bowling alley pavilion with the row house wall to the right, and then using this as a lever, flexing the bulk of the house at an angle to Manhattan's street-grid plan. This created a complex energy rarely seen in urban mansions, at least in New York.

Elizabeth Scriven Clark, who had later married the Right Reverend Henry Codman Potter, the Episcopal bishop of New York, was also interested in housing at the other end of the spectrum, and she built a row of model tenements in which the poor could escape the tyranny of the typical 25-foot-front lot. Flagg organized the buildings, on West 68th and 69th Streets between Amsterdam and West End Avenues (fig. 137), as groups of four in 100-foot-square units, clustered around an interior court, which was meant to offer a civilizing force as it had done at the Dakota. Elizabeth also built a neighborhood settlement house on the Lower East Side, a private stable, and even underwrote trial landscaping of the center malls on Broadway where she purchased a half-dozen large corner lots fronting on the avenue.

While Alfred's widow was branching out on her own, their son Ambrose Clark was making a hesitant attempt to revive the original vision of the Clark estate for the family properties around the Dakota. In 1902 he hired Percy Griffin to design eighteen rowhouses for the south side of 74th Street between Central Park West and Columbus Avenue (fig. 138). Each concrete-floored, fire-proof, five-story house had 17 to 19 rooms and its own dynamo to generate electricity for elevators, a radical innovation in rowhouse construction. Griffin's row emulates London's sophisticated terraces, and in 1906 a writer in the *Architectural Record* noted, "To the passer-by, the block presents an orderly and attractive picture," something Edward Clark had clearly sought two decades before. By this time private houses in New York were facing stiff competition from apartments, and this Clark row had water filters, wine refrigerators, silver safes, and similar details. Plans for the row generally show a butler's room, coal bin, and servant's hall in the basement; kitchen, reception, and billiard room on the first floor; and six or seven servants' bedrooms on the top floor. They were in exquisite taste but backward-looking – impeccably *retardataire*. At the same time Clark put up a dry-goods store at 54 West 74 Street on the Columbus Avenue corner.

It is not clear how the Clarks fared in their investment, but the 74th Street row was their last initiative on the West Side. At about the same time they offered for sale the still-vacant Central Park West block-front just north of the Dakota – although with the restriction that any subsequent building never exceed the height of the Dakota itself. There were no buyers with this demand, and the plot was sold in 1907 with no restriction, when the present Langham apartment building was

FIG. 138. Rowhouses erected by the Clark family at 18 through 52 West 74 Street in 1904
*Wurts Brothers, Museum of the City of New York 33866*

built at 135 Central Park West about four stories higher than the Dakota. This was, in terms of New York City real estate development, the end of the end for the Clarks.

But there was one more architectural event in New York City to come from the family: the mansion of Stephen Carlton Clark, brother of Ambrose, Sterling, and Edward Severin Clark. In 1911 Stephen Clark began a 50-foot wide town house at 46 East 70 Street – now the Explorers Club (fig. 139). He retained a young designer, Frederick Sterner, who had finally, unlike others, been able to reinvent the brownstone rowhouse by amputating the stoops to make a street-level entry, remaking the interiors with double height rooms, and refacing the exteriors in picturesque designs. Sterner's house for Clark has a soaring brick front of restrained neo-Tudor style and large window bays of leaded glass that make its five floors seem like only three. Inside there is access to a raised mid-lot terrace that is a particularly gracious amenity. This is one of the most interesting large houses on the Upper East Side, a fitting close to the legacy of architectural patronage of this remarkable New York family.

FIG. 139. House of Stephen Carlton Clark at 46 East 70 Street in 1913. It is now the home of the Explorers' Club, which had formerly been housed in space within the Majestic Apartments with its entrance across the street from the entrance to the Dakota. *Architecture* Magazine

Fig. 140. The iconic double-dragon-and-wise-man iron casting that alternates with stone piers to support the iron railing around the building's dry moat. *Kenneth Grant*

July 12, 1982      **THE**      Price $1.25

# NEW YORKER

Iris Van Rynbach

FIG. 141. Iris Van Rynbach, *courtesy of Condé Nast Publications*

# CHAPTER 12

# The Dakota as icon

T HE DAKOTA was sufficiently well-known that the visual distinction of its cast-iron railing was used in an early advertisement for the Hecla Iron Works, the company that was responsible for making that railing and other ironwork in the building. Hecla placed an ad in a 1902 issue of Architectural Record magazine (fig. 147), which shows the company's showroom with one of the Dakota's decorative castings in the most prominent position..

It has shown up in such disparate places as the covers of a 1979 *Brentano's* Christmas catalogue and a 1982 issue of *The New Yorker* magazine. And a model of the building in Lego blocks forms a part of Legoland in Florida.

FIG. 142. Christmas catalogue of 1979 for a now-defunct New York bookstore that was already 31 years old when the Dakota opened.

FIG. 143. A 3-inch square pewter replica from InFocus Tech, www.ReplicaBuildings.com

FIG. 144. In anticipation of the millennium, in 1998 Constantin Boym created a series of miniatures titled Buildings of Disaster, the twist of fate in this instance being the tragic shooting and death of John Lennon at the Dakota on 8 December 1980. *Constantin Boym, www.boym.com*

FIG. 145. Tissue box from www.HetStudios. com

FIG. 146. The Dakota in Lego blocks at Legoland, Florida

# HECLA IRON WORKS

(Formerly POULSON & EGER,)

## ARCHITECTURAL AND ORNAMENTAL
## BRONZE AND IRON WORK

Show Rooms at Office Building of the Hecla Iron Works.

## Iron and Bronze Stairs, Railings, Grilles, Elevator Enclosures and Cars

ETC., ETC.

FIG. 147. The Hecla Iron Works cast the specially-designed double-dragon-and-wise-man iron supports for the railing around the building. Those sculptures were so distinctive that the company prominently displayed one in its showroom, and featured the casting in its ads for at least 20 years after.

# CHAPTER 13

# The Dakota in print

A S FAR AS is known, the only other published book about the history of the Dakota is Stephen Birmingham's *Life at the Dakota*, first published in 1979 by Random House. But there are many books that tell something about the building, and a comparable number of newspaper and magazine articles that speak of the building and some of the people who have lived in it. A few of the earliest of such articles are reproduced earlier in this volume and longer ones can be found in the APPENDICES at the end of the book. Here are offered two relatively modern illustrated articles. Both perpetuate the mythical tale about how the Dakota got its name, but both also present useful information and photographs. *The Great Dakota* was published in the 28 July 1964 issue of LOOK Magazine, which existed from February 1937 to October 1971 as a rival to LIFE Magazine. *The venerable Dakota* appeared in the March 1959 issue of Architectural Forum. That professional journal began in 1892 as The Brickbuilder and ceased publication with its issue of March 1974. The writers and photographers for both articles are also dead.

*Gay blades skated below Dakota in the '90's.*

# THE GREAT DAKOTA

THIS NEW YORK CITY landmark, a legend in its lifetime, was Manhattan's first luxury apartment building. Today (right), it is one of the most coveted. To some 100 VIP tenants, the Dakota is more than a home: It is a distinguished, fast-disappearing way of life. Located at 72nd Street and Central Park West, the house was built for Edward Clark, president of the Singer Sewing Machine Co., designed by architect Henry J. Hardenbergh and completed in 1884. The site was then so remote that a friend of Clark's called it Indian territory. "Why don't you build it out in

## This Old World leviathan is more than an apartment house—it's a way of life

Dakota?" he asked. Thus the name. Turreted and gabled, it now houses a galaxy of residents, who, like musicologist-critic Edward Downes at right, still enter and leave through the great arched gateway as doormen attend to their vehicular needs. The massive iron gates are still locked at midnight. A staff of about 30 provides instant maintenance and service. However, like the surroundings, some things at the Dakota have changed. The building has gone cooperative—a growing trend among people who prefer restoring and remaining in the old to moving into the new. Gardens, tennis and croquet courts are gone. The vast wine cellar is empty; the private banquet room and servants' quarters are apartments. But as shown here and following, the genteel fortress, with all its arabesques and iron lace, continues to afford pleasure and privacy for dedicated Dakotans.

**PRODUCED BY CHARLES BAITER    PHOTOGRAPHED BY PHILLIP HARRINGTON**

continued

# DAKOTA

Interiors of the domed Dakota (above) are as individual as the people who live there. Because it was built in the days of rugged individualism, no two apartments are structurally the same. In size, they range from four to 18 rooms. Although all have 15-foot ceilings and virtually soundproof walls, the design details of the elaborate moldings, paneled doors, parquet flooring and carved mantelpieces vary throughout. With this background of spaciousness and style, owners may take off in any decoration direction.

## Apartments are highly personal showcases for the ornate past and the stark present

Dakota decoration often highlights residents' professions. The living room of interior designer-antique dealer Frederick P. Victoria (above) is a showcase for styles of furnishings he endorses. A collector of antique clocks, he owns over 20, which bing and bong through the apartment. The carved wood "draperies," not part of the architecture, are copies of 18th-century originals. In contrast, the gallery-like duplex of artist Giora Novak and his designer wife is severely spare. The living room (left) was once the Dakota's banquet room. The transformation, after two years of remodeling and decorating, is still going on. Mantelpiece, ceiling and stained-glass doors remain, as does the room's character. For even the carpeted walls conform to the Dakota's legacy of luxury.

continued

# DAKOTA

Life at New York's Dakota literally revolves around the fountain-studded courtyard (left). Although the building was designed and constructed to permit the utmost in personal privacy, sociable Dakotans — in a city of mutual indifference — really enjoy each other's company. Talented neighbor-guests at a typical intramural party might include a doctor, lawyer, actress, clergyman, opera star, artist, diplomat, a European prince, even a venerable Dakota-born-and-bred aristocrat. And when the party's over, there is always an easily reachable retreat to retire to just down the corridor or across the courtyard.

## Dakotans respect privacy, but enjoy their parties

*Theater couples like Jason Robards, Jr., and his wife Lauren Bacall (above) and (opposite) the Zachary Scotts (Ruth Ford)* *escape the limelight in the elegant privacy of their apartments. Dakota's West Side location is especially convenient for actors.*

*Guests at party given by Dr. and Mrs. Scott Severns (above) are fellow residents. The skyline view across Central Park is bonus.*

continued

# DAKOTA

## From top to bottom: comfort and style for many tastes and talents

This Victorian-vintage "chateau" is a nine-story maze of imaginative, distinctive living. From the entrance, flanked by urn-bound cherubs (above), to the pinnacled walk-around roof, the Dakota is an opulent setting for its owners. Inside the formidable courtyard gates, four separate entrances lead to a network of sit-down elevators, mahogany-paneled corridors and elaborate iron and marble staircases. For devoted Dakotans, all of these passageways eventually lead to home.

*Activities in the Dakota today are neither stuffy nor staid, despite its grande-dame appearance and solid social history. They reveal busy schedules and sophisticated tastes. Above, in her billiards room, actress-singer Susan Stein coaches neighbor Mrs. Aschwin de Lippe. At right, writer Walter Millis and his columnist wife Eugenia Sheppard catch up on each other's worlds in the library of their first-floor apartment. Designer Ward Bennett (far right) uses remodeled servants' quarters in the eaves as a sumptuous studio.*

# The venerable Dakota

PHOTOGRAPHS BY GEORGE CSERNA

## Gallery

One spring day in 1879, lawyer Edward Clark, president of the Singer sewing machine company, took lunch with a group of his fellow executives and financiers on Wall Street. In those days midtown New York was located at about 23rd Street; 52nd Street, where William K. Vanderbilt was about to build a mansion, was considered far uptown. It was a jocose lunch, but the biggest joke of the gathering by far was Clark's announcement that he had decided to build an elegant rental "apartment" on the west side of William Cullen Bryant's new Central Park—way up on 72nd Street. "West 72nd Street," one of the diners exclaimed, "that's still Indian territory, isn't it? Why don't you go a few blocks more and build it out in Dakota?" "That's a good name," said Clark, and smiled one of his rare smiles.

Two years later, and eight years before either North or South Dakota was admitted to the Union, the Dakota opened its elegant doors. In a day when apartment houses were just beginning to be accepted, the Dakota was New York's most lavish—its site cost $250,000 and the structure $2 million. An Indian head was carved on the façade.

The 100-apartment Dakota is still there. It still has the same mahogany woodwork, and the Clark family still owns it. It continues to be beautifully maintained. Its masonry walls and partitions are so thick that it stays cool in summer. In its capacious caverns underground are the same hydraulic elevator reservoirs and the same steam plant that once manufactured heat for buildings for blocks around. The apartments are immense by today's standards, and there is still a long waiting list of eager prospective tenants.

The Dakota's architect was Henry Janeway Hardenbergh, then 32, of New Jersey, great-great grandson of a founder of Rutgers. His style was derived from the various beloved bourgeois styles of the nineteenth century (Victorian, pseudo-Gothic, Brewery Brick), and he later built such imposing structures in New York as the Plaza Hotel, the Waldorf, and the Astoria—but none of these were to receive the same loving care over the years as the Dakota. Gone are the beautiful gardens and croquet and tennis courts once maintained in the adjoining block on grounds which are now used for a commercial parking space. But the Dakota still has a moat between it and the sidewalk, and the iron grille to the courtyard entrance closes at midnight; the visitor or resident rings for entrance after that.

*Most apartments viewing on Central Park were designed with four bedrooms, one bath (with a wooden bathtub), drawing room, library, reception room, kitchen, butler's pantry, maid's room, and bath. They rented for $6,000 to $7,000 per year then—and, remarkably, still do now.*

123

Entrance to the courtyard, with
its iron gate open and sentry
on duty, gives the appearance of
a fortress entry. Inside the court
are four separate entrances to
elevator lobbies. The structure
of this massive building is wall-
bearing, with steel arches.
Shown to the right is a detail
of the sidewalk railing.

124

THE VENERABLE DAKOTA

*Two fountains in the interior*
*courtyard serve also as*
*ventilators and skylights for*
*a large basement service space*
*below. Service elevators*
*(the first in New York) were placed*
*between the backs of the apartments*
*(diagram below). Carriages*
*once rolled into the court, but*
*automobiles are barred today.*

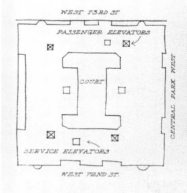

WEST 73RD ST

PASSENGER ELEVATORS

COURT

CENTRAL PARK WEST

SERVICE ELEVATORS

WEST 72ND ST.

*The Dakota's bedrooms (above) are quiet. Floor*
*slabs are parquet on boards on sleepers*
*over 9 inches of earth (for*
*acoustical insulation) and 9 inches*
*of concrete. Today's tenants include a number*
*of diplomats, publishers, and theater people:*
*e.g., actresses Judy Holliday, Teresa Wright,*
*Ruth Ford, actors José Ferrer,*
*Boris Karloff, Zachary Scott, designer*
*Jo Mielziner, and playwright Sidney Kingsley.*

126

A classic column replaces bearing partitions in
the building's largest drawing room
(24 feet by 49 feet). This room is in the
apartment of publisher C. D. Jackson. Ceilings
are 15½ feet high on the first floor
diminishing to 12 feet on the eighth. Original
detailing, such as the plaster ceiling (right) is
in immaculate condition. Above, right, is a
detail of one of the laminated sliding
doors, showing an original glass insert.

Stairway in the first-floor
public hall is typical of the
building's richly ornamental ironwork.
The building is still heated
by the original steam radiators
(which, in apartments, are built
in under the window sills).
It is a two-pipe system, with an
added line: under each radiator
in the apartments is a pan to
catch any seepage, and from the
pans a network of drainage lines
runs down to cisterns in the
basement which also receive
roof water. This water originally
was used in the building's
own steam plant, which is on
stand-by status now, and for
the hydraulic elevators. Two
of the reservoirs for these
are shown at right.

128

THE VENERABLE DAKOTA

*Mahogany-finished elevator cab, installed by Otis Brothers in 1880, is the oldest in New York City. To care for the Dakota there are 52 employees; the building is managed by Horace S. Ely & Company under the careful eye of Matthew G. Ely Jr. Below is a panel typical of the instrumentation in the mechanical rooms in the basement: steamboat character, complete with polished brass.*

**END**

# CHAPTER 14

# Dakota apartments and their residents

A S ALMOST EVERY article about the Dakota will tell you, much of its renown derives from its stellar list of *dramatis personae*. While on that score this book may disappoint by not providing the juicy tales and tabloid gossip, several now-departed former residents maintained distinctive apartments in the building that received journalistic coverage while they were alive. As a way of offering images of some very different life styles that the Dakota has supported, on the following pages are reproduced these articles:

RUDOLF NUREYEV *The Nutcracker Suite: Rudolf Nureyev's Dakota apartment was a baroque setting for the dramatic gesture*, by Suzanne Slesin, photos by Oberto Gili, The New York Times Sunday Magazine, 20 September 1993.

GIORA NOVAK *At Home in the Dakota*, by Olga Gueft, photos by Louis Reens, Interiors Magazine

WARD BENNETT *A Rooftop Eyrie gives a modern designer exactly the home he wants*, photos by Jon Naar, House & Garden, © Condé Nast February 1965

WARD BENNETT *Rooms at the top*, by Martin Filler, photos by Henry Wolf and George Cserna, Progressive Architecture, July 1979, courtesy of Hanley Wood. This article shows the renovation 15 years later of the original 1964 scheme for Bennett's roof-top apartment. He had moved into the Dakota in 1942.

DESIGN

BY SUZANNE SLESIN

# THE NUTCRACKER SUITE

RUDOLF NUREYEV'S DAKOTA
APARTMENT WAS A BAROQUE SETTING
FOR THE DRAMATIC GESTURE.

THEY ARE ROOMS OF SUCH DRAMA AND
sweep that Nureyev must have felt right at
home: 14-foot ceilings, massive windows
and doors and a collection of old-master paintings —
huge in size, heroic in subject — that lends the place
the air of a late-19th-century art salon.

Rudolf Nureyev's six-room pied-à-terre in the
Dakota — one of seven homes he owned — was a
repository for the dancer's acquisitive ways. When he
died in January at 54, the choreographer and collector had amassed thousands of works of art, textiles,

*An Elizabethan oak-and-marquetry*
*tester bed is the focus of Nureyev's ornate master bedroom.*
*Note the rolled-up kilims peeking out from under*
*the bed and the fabric remnants draped over an*
*Italian Renaissance chest. Textiles were the dancer's passion,*
*and he collected them all over the world.*

STYLIST: JEFFREY W. MILLER

sculptures, maps, prints, costumes and furniture, which will be sold by Christie's in 1995 to benefit two dance foundations.

The New York apartment, purchased in 1982 and rarely lived in, has the quality of a three-dimensional scrapbook. The 3,300-square-foot space — with its vast, dimly lighted rooms, opening off a long, dark hall — is faded yet grand. None of the usual conventions apply. The kitchen looks as if it was hardly used. There are few closets. Only Victorian shutters, original to the apartment, cover the mahogany-framed windows through which Nureyev, a man who hated air-conditioning and other modern amenities, could glimpse the treetops of Central Park.

The cavernous living room is dominated by allegorical paintings, hung frame to frame like postage stamps affixed to an album. Velvet-covered sofas that once belonged to Maria Callas and a Russian settee languish like wallflowers at the ball. In the center, there is a first-century Roman marble torso, one of Nureyev's favorite possessions.

Theatricality is the leitmotif of the haphazard décor. The music room is dominated by a 10-foot organ. The dining room is covered in scenic hand-painted Chinese wallpaper. An immense Venetian glass chandelier — so large it had to be hoisted through the windows — explodes like a fireworks display, in sharp contrast to the stark suite of early-20th-century Thonet chairs by Josef Urban.

Wherever he traveled, Nureyev shopped relentlessly, bringing home Indian shawls and Japanese obis, 18th-century maps, costumes and stage memorabilia with the zeal of a hunter who pauses just long enough to put down his bounty before setting off again. Possession was all, display an afterthought.

The master bedroom, papered in a dark floral pattern, is crammed with carpets and textiles. Rolled-up kilims, tags still affixed, peek out from under the Elizabethan carved bed, while remnants of antique fabric spill over an Italian Renaissance chest.

"He was obviously a very tactile person, not a pallid, anemic esthete," says Peter Watson, who has been visiting Nureyev's many homes for a biography. Watson attributes Nureyev's predilection for pattern and texture to his Russian background. And his obsessive accumulation of houses and things may have been a reaction to a childhood spent in a one-room house in the Urals. But on Central Park West, in a setting eccentric and grand, the possessions are a backdrop for the portrait of a sensuous man.

ABOVE:
*A first-century Roman marble torso commands the cavernous living room. A portrait of Lord de Ferrars by Sir Joshua Reynolds hangs over the fireplace. Behind the door there is a late-18th-century allegorical painting by Johann Heinrich Fuseli.*

RIGHT:
*Under Charles Meynier's 19th-century painting "Wisdom Defending Youth Against Love" there is a neo-classical Russian settee upholstered in lavender silk and adorned in ormolu.*

PHOTOGRAPHS BY OBERTO GILI FOR THE NEW YORK TIMES

ABOVE: *Dominating the dining room is a*
*Venetian chandelier of Murano glass. The 17th-century table*
*is surrounded by a set of Josef Urban side chairs.*
*The wallpaper is hand-painted Chinese, mounted on linen.*
RIGHT: *At the core of the apartment is this long*
*wood-paneled hall. At one end is an anteroom with leather*
*wallpaper and a marble male torso.*

PHOTOGRAPHS BY OBERTO GILI FOR THE NEW YORK TIMES

## AT HOME IN THE DAKOTA

*Giora and Judy Novak meet the challenge of grand scale
in an apartment where space to live, work, entertain, and display paintings
was to be had for the organizing*

Amid the jerry-built structures of our Kleenex civilization, the Dakota is a symbol of stability. Its apartments are even more desirable today than when it rose west of Central Park in 1881. No one then minded the 72nd Street location (as remote as Indian territory — whence its name), any more than anyone today cares that its address still lacks east side *cachet*. When the building went cooperative two years ago, no one complained about the Victorian-brewery- Gothic exterior concocted by Henry Janeway Hardenbergh (who later designed the Plaza). What mattered were the eternal verities of its huge rooms, mahogany woodwork, and walls and ceilings packed with two feet of earth to insulate and to muffle sound. The meticulously maintained building was hardly altered even then, except that servants were dispossessed from

the rooms under the eaves to make saleable penthouses. A tenant restaurant on the first floor was also dismantled with its basement adjunct. Among the most nobly scaled in the building, this potential apartment lacked baths, kitchen, closets, even doors and walls at openings from the public corridors. Only an aged millionaire with an army of servants could be expected to take the unwieldy rental package. But is it a young couple who have it now, and maintain it with one part-time helper.

Israeli-born artist Giora Novak wanted precisely what it offered — studio space for huge paintings, sculptures, and constructions, storage space for the books and paraphernalia of a lifetime, wall space to display paintings, space for life and friends . . . space, in other words, for his permanent home. He is convinced that New

York is the world's art center and where he will always want to be.

As an experienced interior designer, Judy Novak, Giora's Chicago-born wife of three years, had the task of converting the raw space to the purpose. However, the appalling size and hard reverberations from the marble floor prompted her to ask the advice of Philip Johnson. He pronounced the double-square proportions of the main room magnificent, prescribed carpeted walls to deal with the noise problem, and suggested as little tampering as possible. After that he left her to her own devices, and with the exception of consultation on lighting from Richard Kelly, it is only Judy Novak's spare, subtly adjusted, but boldly scaled devices that are illustrated here, among the decorative sculptural flourishes of the building and her husband's ultra-abstract sculpture and painting.—*O. G.*

*View from bedroom doors to living-dining room, in other words from the former restaurant's smaller to its larger dining hall. Mahogany doors with stained glass panels and coffered mahogany ceiling have not been molested except for a careful cleaning and dark rubbing to tone down the red overtones. Also unimproved is the marble floor with inlaid border in green, black and red marble, and the huge carved brownstone chimney. Black marble dadoes were removed to thread outlets, then replaced. Mahogany wall paneling has been replaced with inexpensive off-white carpeting over strips to support Giora Novak's painting, which can thus be frequently changed without leaving punctures.*

58

photographs by louis reens

*Sparse but large-scaled furniture is grouped in symmetrical squares to define conversation and dining areas. Dining and coffee tables are topped with identical 5½" marble squares, the only difference being height. Flanked by the two sofas, coffee table is used for dining also, and can in addition be rimmed by low Japanese chairs. Squared off sofas are low but beefed up with double layer of cushioning to cope with scale of the space.*

59

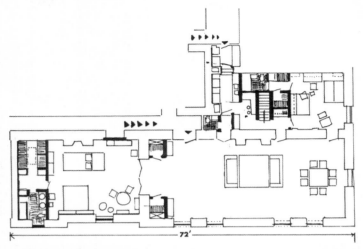

Plan of street floor *indicates where new walls close the gaps between public corridor and the former dining rooms that the Novaks converted into their home. Conveniently centralized kitchen-pantry-bar area has two service exits of its own. Master bath, dressing room, powder room near bar-pantry area, guest bath near library-guest room, the kitchen, and a pair of closets between master bedroom and living room (one houses the air-conditioning apparatus) were installed by the Novaks. Ceiling on the main floor are 15½ feet high.*
*Lower floor plan (not shown) roughly follows the same outline as the upper, but is divided into only two rooms—a huge studio and smaller storage-file room.*

Photo top left: *Mouse on brownstone mantel pilaster.*
Photo center left: *In vast basement studio: work table, Hardoy chairs, foam-mattress-topped lounge platform, enough lights for painting at any hour.*
Photo bottom left: *Giora Novak's sculpture: stainless steel and glass (above), movable square stainless tubes twixt layers of glass (below).*
Photo above: *Dakota chief on brownstone chimney panel below mahogany ceiling coffers. Judy Novak designed outsize black globe fixtures for outsize space. Richard Kelly was lighting consultant. Edison Price made can spotlights. Kliegl made globes; studio lights are by Beaux-Arts. (Complete source list appears on page 62.)*

Above: *In marble-floored, white carpet-walled main room, the decor changes as Giora Novak's paintings are changed (black-and-white photography camouflages a large pale blue painting between tall window and door). Or—for major room redo, Judy Novak has only to replace sofa fabric—purple Haitian cotton with grap warp nub (Scotchgarded, latex-backed). Giora's sculpture of stainless steel and lucite stands beside sofa.*

At left: *Tall Giora Novak has red-gold hair, Slavic features. His work has been shown at the Venice Bienale, and he has designed buildings (not realized)—one of which* INTERIORS *will present in future. He also designs jewelry.*

61

AT HOME IN THE DAKOTA

62

*Largest painting in bedroom (opposite) is one of few which "reads" in black-and-white photos. Called "Experience of the Little Hours," it was painted by Giora in an Israeli kibbutz in 1960. Within a thin black outer frame the canvas projects about an inch, is primed with stained brown primer; smooth lighter planes of the composition are paled with white films applied by a palette knife (Giora has abandoned brushwork). Currently his painting has become even more abstract, reducing to their most elemental terms the essential components of visual experience . . . the varied tints of imperfect antique glass panes . . . the refracted lines seen in an unfocussed microscope. He studies each theme in "families" of paintings which he works on simultaneously.*

*A smaller Dakota dining room became the Novak's bedroom. As in the rest of the apartment, its marble floor is bare (except for flat, russety horsehide square at carved brownstone hearth); and its walls are muffled in inexpensive warm-white cotton-loop carpet over wall strips that support the paintings. Vertical blinds at the lofty windows cope with sky glare. When open the blinds reveal the unusually high sills and elaborate darkened brass scrollwork below which hide the Dakota's recessed radiators.*

*Judy made subtle and unobtrusive changes: The fine old hardware appears untouched; actually the brass has been darkened so as not to jog the quiet background. The planters are stock designs; yet they are in a special brown-shadowed black finish and are dropped closer to the floor on lowered feet.*

*Multi-colored Alexander Girard stripes— one fine, one broad—cover Saarinen "womb" settee and ottomans and bed. Bertoia chairs are in black Naugahyde. Round cat's-cradle marble-topped tables —the smaller a coffee table and the larger a desk-dining table—are visually transparent yet firmly stable.*

*Much of Judy's knoll and Herman Miller furniture dates back to Judy's years as an interior designer, when she worked for Leonard Linn in Chicago, her home town. Trained at Pembroke College (Brown University) and Illinois Tech's Institute of Design, Judy is widely traveled, met Giora in Israel in 1960. The couple lived in Paris about a year before settling in New York.*

AT HOME IN THE DAKOTA

SOURCES
*Dining and coffee tables:* Laverne Originals (special 5½′ square, black-finish base)
*Chairs:* Laverne Originals (special black-finish bases, special dark-brown leather)
*Sofa:* Made by Dunbar to Judy Novak's design. *Sofa fabric:* Far Eastern
*Vertical blinds:* Louverdrape Vertical Blind Corporation through CBS Venetian and Vertical Blind Company
*Seating and tables in bedroom:* Knoll

*Bed and bedroom case furniture:* Herman Miller. *Fabrics in bedroom:* Herman Miller
*Horsehide rugs:* Hides from Leathers Best, sewing by Harry Hertzman
*Lighting globes, can spotlights, studio spotlights:* manufactured by Edison Price, Kliegl, and Beaux Arts to Judy Novak's design in consultation with Richard Kelly
*Standing and portable lamps:* George Kovacs (modified to Judy Novak's design)

*In this night view of the dining area the vertical blinds are closed flat and the highly versatile lighting system picks out the paintings, plants, and table top. Giora Novak's two square paintings are variations on a theme of russet lines on off-white background, and the deeply carved teak frames are integral to their design. Dining furniture has special black-finished bases, special dark brown leather.*

64

PHOTOGRAPHS BY JON NAAR

# A ROOFTOP EYRIE gives a modern designer exactly the home he wants

To search for an apartment with sun and vista in the heart of New York City is very much like looking for a needle in a haystack. Sun and vista, however, were the goals of interior designer Ward Bennett when he was hunting for a new apartment after his old one had been robbed of its East River view. Mr. Bennett also had a very definite idea of *how* he wanted to live, a manner which he termed "purely in the twentieth century." Specifically, this meant an end to traditional backgrounds because "we do not lead traditional lives," the ruling out of "dark brownstones" and the quest for a studio environment, the kind artists have cherished for centuries.

Remarkably, Mr. Bennett was able to stake out his new way of life in one of the oldest apartment buildings in New York, the famous septuagenarian château on Central Park West called the Dakota. There, on the rooftop, he bought a two-story cluster of servants' quarters that included, on the first floor, four bedroom cubicles-with-sinks ranged around an airshaft, a hall leading to a public bath and toilet, a backdoor staircase leading to a single second-story room and a two-story skylight painted black. With an expert's technical knowledge and a romantic's perception, he set about transforming this dismal miscellany into the sky-and-sun-filled studio apartment he lives and works in today.

Two cubicles and a piece of a public corridor he turned into a fluid living-dining area (see plan, *below*), ripping out the cubicle sinks as he went along. Into the once public hall he installed a compact kitchen, and a third bedroom he converted into a gallery (for art and after-dinner coffee). From the single existing bathroom, cut off now from its former hall, a door was cut through into a newly installed lavatory which in turn leads to the only bedroom the designer left unaltered. For the living room he designed and built a new staircase that wings, like a stabile sculpture, up to the second-story crow's nest where he has set up his office.

Mr. Bennett has also courted ardently the light and vista he values so highly. By painting the walls around the airshaft white, and covering the airshaft itself with pewter-colored subway grating, he has created the illusion of a courtyard where he places stone sculpture and plants. The old-fashioned double-hung windows have been replaced by plain glass in pivot frames. He has also added two new windows and replaced the skylight's murky panes. The new concrete floor of the upper-level studio was designed to stop a few feet short of the outside wall so that the living room's huge skylight could ascend uninterrupted almost to the peak of the room above.

The original rooftop entrance has been retained and through it a sense of space, air and greenery seems to flow right into the apartment. It is sparingly but distinctively furnished with such disparate pieces as a luxurious Italian marble dining table and an adjustable Victorian iron deck chair. And every room is enhanced with art—contemporary drawings, gouaches, antique carvings, pre-Columbian sculpture.

Main floor of Ward Bennett's rooftop apartment revolves around an airshaft as some houses circle a courtyard. On one side a gallery leads from the corner-to-corner living-dining room to bedroom and bath. On the other side of the shaft is the kitchen. Staircase spirals to upper-level studio.

UPPER LEVEL
Office
Entrance
Dining area
Kitchen
Air shaft
Bath
Lav.
Living area
Gallery
Bedroom
LOWER LEVEL

The gallery, a quiet spot for reading during the day, is often used as a withdrawing room for after-dinner coffee. Tray is set on carpeted shelf turned buffet, while Mr. Bennett's guests make themselves comfortable on floor cushions. Next to bedroom doorway hangs a seventeenth-century German roadside Christ.

*Continued*

HOUSE & GARDEN, FEBRUARY, 1965

From the adjoining roof, *below,* the apartment looks like two lopsided pyramids joined by a bridge. Skylight rises from one end of living room to studio above. Small windows are in gallery and bedroom. Rooftop entrance is on other side of center bridge. *Bottom of page:* living room in three stages of reconstruction.

In the kitchen, *below,* all appliances are ranged along one wall, all are enameled black. Closet at end replaces usual wall-hung cabinets. Radiator covered with subway-grille serves as plate warmer and buffet. Kitchen by Dwyer.

Living room, *above,* is roughly divided by a great buttress-like chimney, into dining area at left, reading-and-conversation area at right. Centered on the chimney is a bronze by Reg Butler. A pair of mattresses covered in glove leather stand in for a sofa, and the amber tones of its pillows are accented by a string of amber beads hanging on the wall. Steel and leather sled chair is Bennett's own design. Sliced arch of doorway to gallery, *right,* is remnant of original construction, but looks like a modern tour de force.

Living and dining areas, *below,* are related by continuous shelf for pictures and art objects along room's longest wall. Steel I-beams frame wall space and windows.

*Continued*

Bedroom, *below*, and bathroom *right*, are like a single L-shaped room although the tub and toilet section may be closed off with a floor-to-ceiling door. Tall windows on bathroom leg of L are fitted with shades that roll up from bottom to afford privacy without cutting off light. Bed is covered with black fabric. A camphor chest topped with a bright red Early American tray serves as a night table.

Lavatory, *above* and *left*, is completely new addition to the apartment since existing bathroom had none. Whole back wall of alcove is lined with mirror and luminescent panel lights it from above. Just beyond is corner of bedroom near door to gallery.

In bathroom proper, *above*, old fixtures were retained because the designer likes their old-fashioned lines. The outside of the tub is painted Delphinium Blue. Plants stand on the quarry tile floor, an ink drawing by Nell Blaine hangs on the wall above the chair, which is an old Rolls Royce jump seat. Shower curtain is made of classic raincoat fabric. The telephone plugs into a jack at window sill to the left.

Floor of upstairs room was demolished, *above*, and replaced with a new one of concrete, leaving space at one side, *above right*, so that skylight (and ivy) could rise continuously from living room below up to studio ceiling.

The studio, *below*, Mr. Bennett's preferred workroom, (he has another in mid-town), has ample space for files, books and blueprints. One work table has a top of oak butcher block, the other is covered in black leather. Tufted leather chair is a Bennett design. Floor is covered with white mosaic tiles.

Interior design: Bennett apartment, New York

# Rooms at the top

**Designer Ward Bennett's own apartment atop New York's fabled, gabled Dakota is a distillation of his philosophy of minimal, carefully crafted interiors.**

The names of the residents at the legendary Dakota apartments in New York read like the passenger list of an incredible voyage onward and upward with the arts: John Lennon, Paul Goldberger, Rex Reed, Leonard Bernstein, Lauren Bacall, and other glitterati too numerous to mention all live in the landmark structure. But up on the roof lives a man whose tenancy long predates the Dakota's relatively recent rise to chic. Ward Bennett, the bearded guru of a whole younger generation of interior designers (P/A, Sept. 1978, p. 82) has lived at the Dakota since 1942. And for the past 15 of those years, he has occupied—and has just renovated—a unique collection of spaces within the central, pyramidal gable that overlooks Central Park.

Built in 1884 to the designs of Henry J. Hardenbergh, the Dakota is like that architect's other major New York landmark, the Plaza Hotel, in that its interior spaces tend to be either wonderful or horrendous. The odd, left-over rooms beneath the Dakota's picturesque roofline were long thought to fit into that latter category. Originally, the gables were designed to be the province of servant girls and scullery maids. But to Ward Bennett, who bought the main garret in 1962 when the building became a cooperative, it was an opportunity to create a distinctive apartment that has become, in the past decade and a half, an ever-changing, but always consistent, expression of his approach to design.

### 5 rms, prk vu

Access to the Bennett apartment is, by usual New York standards, rather astonishing. Halfway through a journey that in-

Bennett apartment is located in central gable of landmark Dakota building overlooking Central Park. Designer acquired garret in 1962.

George Cserna

cludes mazelike corridors, elevators, and stairways, one wonders whether one ought to have left behind a trail of pebbles in order to retrace the tortuous route. Finally, one passes through a door—outside again, onto the roof of the building! But momentary consternation fades as the visitor gains sight of the breath-catching vista that lies below: Central Park, and its Lake (spanned by Calvert Vaux's graceful Bow Bridge), set off by the limestone backdrop of Fifth Ave. This is surely one of the great views of New York.

The contradictory aspects of the Dakota roofscape are inescapable: it is at once as quaint as some Graustarkian duchy, but it is quite powerful, too, in the strong geometry of its forms. Small wonder that it has great appeal to Ward Bennett, whose own work, despite its seeming simplicity, is suffused with a certain ambiguity of contrasting forces. Most emblematic of that condition is the Dakota's enormous flagpole, which becomes a dominant indoor/outdoor part of Bennett's scheme, and which also neatly summarizes his attitude toward design.

The flagpole plunges down through the apex of the gable pyramid. Inside, in his upper-level study, Bennett has appropriated the flagpole's ample girth as the base of a table, made by adding a circular wooden plane to complete what the existing elements had already started. Craning one's head near the dramatic, two-story studio window that dominates the north slope of the pyramid, one can catch a foreshortened glimpse of the Stars and Stripes billowing overhead, a bright splash of primary colors amidst the black and white. Devoid of the iconic significance it would attain at the hands of a Venturi or a Moore, the flag here becomes just another striking design element, incorporated without special reference to its meaning. This almost studied neutrality is at the heart of Bennett's style, a style that does not seek to conceal its artfulness (as some have supposed), but which rather leaves it up to the viewer to discern what was intended, and what was not.

This happens throughout the apartment. In the living room is Bennett's desk, which at first glance looks like a Gurney for the very rich: black stone slab on a tubular chrome base with large black rubber casters. One assumes that this is an appropriated piece of hospital equipment, but no—it was custom-made to Bennett's own design. It is preferable, to be sure, to an ormolu-encrusted *bureau-plat,* but its associational references do intrude into our reaction to it, whether or not its designer so intended. Entering the apartment from the roof, one is confronted by a pair of striking metal sculptures. These vertical, deeply fluted, hourglass shapes (reminiscent of the rough-hewn wooden bases Brancusi crafted for his own sculpture)

Upper level study is open on one side to living room below (opposite page). Two-story studio window frames view of roof and Central Park.

**Bennett apartment**

Ward Bennett

Bedroom (above left) is reached through gallery (above right) connecting with living room (right). Low, narrow archway entrance to bedroom (above right) reflects shape of original arched window at right. Sense of compression created by archway makes relatively small bedroom seem initially larger by contrast, a device often used by Frank Lloyd Wright. In living room (right), seating was kept deliberately low to compensate for sloping walls.

SECOND FLOOR

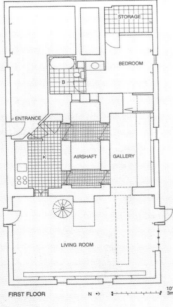

FIRST FLOOR

turn out, conversely, not to be *objêts d'art,* but *objêts trouvés:* they are actually cogwheels used to strip bark from logs at lumber mills.

**I'm looking through you**
To one side of this entry area is an aligned series of windows. The first two windows flank an air shaft, over which Bennett has set a nonstructural deck of industrial grating, in order to cut the sense of an abyss below. On the other side of the air shaft is a gallery with a similar alignment of two windows, which in turn lead the eye into the apartment again, and then out the other side of the pyramid. This intriguing visual sequence of indoor and outdoor spaces verges on the illusionistic. One then passes through the kitchen, which is barely recognizable as such, since there are few signs of the preparation or consumption of food (save for some Bennett-designed utensils). This immaculate galley is a great deal neater than many formal entrance foyers.

Next comes the living room, which extends along the full width of the gable. Its

steeply sloping walls clearly define the exterior shape of the pyramid. In explaining his original remodeling of the space, Bennett says, "I stripped away everything I could which would still leave the place standing." He acceded to the strong diagonal thrust of the existing space in a number of ways. The emphatic slant of the flagpole base in the living room is the mirror opposite of that of the walls, and it occupies a position in the room that approximates that of a fireplace in conventional interiors. Seating in the room is kept deliberately low: the usual chairs and sofas would have made the space seem a great deal smaller. A vaguely Oriental feeling is heightened by an exquisite Cambodian head of Buddha, resting horizontally on a round black pillow, the color of its stone echoed most closely by the gray-beige wall-to-wall carpeting that is used throughout living room, gallery, and bedroom.

The gallery connecting living room and bedroom is little more than a walkway, save for its low shelf, on which are displayed framed drawings and etchings by

Le Corbusier, Picasso and Miró. Beyond is the bedroom, which some might find a bit stark. Its bed, draped in black leather, looks rather uninviting. Here the uncomplicated ease of the rest of the apartment gives way to a stringent sense of denial. The adjacent bathroom, though, is a fine corrective to the mirrored and marbled excesses of "decorator" remodelings. The original ball-and-claw-foot bathtub is here, and what must be the world's most famous towel rack: Bennett's black tubular steel man-hole surround, widely published as part of the High Tech craze.

But the best room of all is at the very top. From a circular stairway in the living room, one ascends to a small study, with white walls and white tile floor, carved out of the top third of the pyramid. A wall of books, some light oak Bennett chairs surrounding the circular table, lush plants, art objects, and that glorious view all combine to make this a special and solitary retreat. Sitting there, Ward Bennett must certainly feel that it has been well worth the climb to the top. [Martin Filler]

**Data**
**Project:** Bennett apartment, New York.
**Interior design:** Ward Bennett.
**Program:** renovation of two-level apartment for owner-designer.
**Major materials:** steel and plaster walls, tile and carpeted floors.
**Client:** Ward Bennett.
**Cost:** withheld at request of client.
**Photography:** Henry Wolf, except as noted.

Spiral stairway in living room (top right) leads to upper level study (top left). Dakota flagpole is incorporated to create table by addition of circular wooden top. Flagpole is anchored in massive diagonal base in center of living room (top right). Low seating, precisely framed landscape views, and Oriental art objects (right) give living room an Eastern feeling.

# CHAPTER 15

# Keeping the Dakota in good repair

A S HUMANS AGE, their physical ailments tend to increase with the attendant costs of alleviating them. Buildings are not much different, except that the ways in which they make their problems known are non-verbal. An old man can complain that his internal plumbing system is hurting, thereby prompting an investigation of the cause. But an old building with deteriorating plumbing makes its problems known only by leaking, or sometimes by catastrophic failure. The Dakota is a very old building. When it was owned by the Clark family, maintenance and repairs were attended to in private (or ignored) with no one to whom the family had to answer. In 1961, ownership passed to a cooperative corporation, owned by all the building's residents who had both a personal and a financial interest in repairs and their cost. In 1969, the New York City Landmarks Preservation Commission designated the Dakota as a protected landmark, which brought an added layer of scrutiny to all maintenance and repair work to the exterior of the building, even if the repairs couldn't be seen from the street.

In 1974, with more than a dozen years' experience of being responsible for the upkeep of the building, the co-op board recognized that a variety of problems would have to be addressed. Loose and occasionally falling slate tiles on the steeply-sloping roofs, and failing copper trim, had caused rain to leak into the building. Plumbing problems were causing other leaks, and the original hydraulic elevators needed work. Cast-iron chimney caps had broken off, and much of the stonework needed attention. That year, the Landmarks Commission approved work that was anticipated to cost upwards of $500,000, and which would require an assessment averaging about $5,000 per apartment. At the time, the board decided that it would delay cleaning the building's façade, which would have doubled the assessment to a figure that the residents would consider unacceptable.

Twenty years later, major repairs to the building envelope were again needed, and this time the entire façade was cleaned. This made it easier to match brick and stone colors in the places where patches and replacements were needed. And this time the problems of the building's 2000 windows were addressed. Repairs were made, and sashes that were beyond repair were replaced to standards that the Landmarks Commission had established. The work was done on the basis of unit pricing, because the scope of the work could be developed only as the job progressed. Cleaning brick cost $4.50 per square foot, removing existing face brick cost $45.00 per square foot, and providing and installing new brick to match the original was an additional $50.00 per square foot. Where the board in 1974 felt that an assessment of $10,000 per apartment would be too much for the residents to support, two decades later the cost averaged out to about $50,000 per apartment to pay for the $5 million renovation.

Later, a decision was made to make all the fireplaces functional again. Tiny electronic cameras were threaded down each of the hundreds of chimney flues (a separate one for each fireplace) and the problem areas recorded on a special set of drawings. Because the unlined brick flues were already of minimal size for the fireplace openings, standard, flexible flue-liners could not be used. Instead, where there were danger spots the flues were completely rebuilt by hand, working from inside each room, with a specially-skilled contractor removing the over-mantels and cabinetry, peeling back the wall coverings, breaking into the walls to reach the flues, and then re-plastering and restoring everything in each room following completion of the brickwork repairs and mortar repointing.

Fast-forward to 2004, and another major reconstruction project was necessary, but this time confined to the central courtyard. The surface of the courtyard had been replaced, apparently several times, with the current covering being a rubberized material that was textured to mimic rough stone. It was leaking badly, allowing rainwater to corrode the hidden steelwork that was supporting the floor of the courtyard. A steel and glass breezeway added in the 1920s to shelter the residents walking through the courtyard to the individual corner elevator lobbies was so rusted that it was said to be held together by its coating of paint alone. For this project, all the old material was removed (leaving in place the two original cast iron fountains that served as skylights for the service courtyard immediately below). The corroded structural steel below was repaired, reinforced, or replaced as needed. A new reinforced-concrete support slab was poured, a complete membrane of waterproofing was installed, and then a new courtyard floor was set in place. This posed an interesting challenge for the building, its architects, and even the Landmarks Commission, as there were neither photographs nor architectural drawings to show what the original materials or their appearance had been. Relying solely on the other original materials still in place around the building, the architects, the contractors, and the co-op board devised a scheme that the Landmarks Commission found acceptable; the entrance and driveway surface, originally intended for horse-drawn carriages, would be made up of granite pavers, similar to the Belgian blocks (commonly called cobblestones) that can still be seen as street paving in parts of the Tribeca area of lower Manhattan. The sidewalk for pedestrians was made up of huge slabs of stone from upstate New York similar to the bluestone used originally for the sidewalk around the building. Those slabs were up to six feet long and five inches thick, with a rounded integral curbstone edge. The entire project took almost a year to complete and is described is the following article that was published in November 2004 in *Stone World*, an industry publication.

# New York landmark gets a new courtyard

*Glacier Blue™ Devonian Stone was chosen for the renovation of the
Dakota apartment complex's courtyard in New York City*

by Michelle Stinnard

Renovation of the Dakota courtyard in New York City included the implementation of Devonian Stone and Iridian granite pavers throughout the sidewalks, driveways and each of the four quadrants of the courtyard.

February 2004 marked the beginning of a 7 ½-month-long renovation of the courtyard at the famous Dakota apartment building in New York City. Originally built in 1884 by Architect Henry Hardenbergh, the legendary edifice is a massive, fortress-like structure with a large center courtyard and over 100 apartment units. Manhattan-based architect, John Wender of Bartolone Wender Architects, was chosen to conduct the restoration of the courtyard. He in turn brought James R. Gainfort AIA Consulting Architects on board for masonry and waterproofing expertise. And when work was completed, stone from New York met the design goals and practical challenges.

According to Catherine Paplin, who managed the project in Gainfort's office, the goal of the project was two-fold. "On the one hand, there was the desire to restore the courtyard to its original spirit, and to whatever extent possible, its original materials and look," said Paplin. "On the other hand, there was simply the desire to make the courtyard beautiful, with a quality of design, workmanship and materials that befit this landmark.

[ 163 ]

The architects chose Glacier Blue™ Devonian stone for much of the paving because of its quality and high level of structural integrity. It also tied well with the historical design of the building.

The stone paving was specified in a broad range of shapes and sizes.

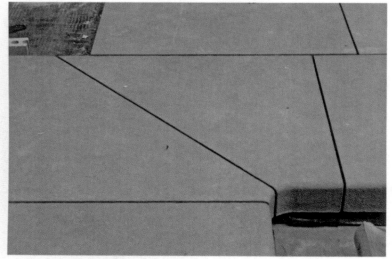

For the corners, the Devonian stone had to be cut at varying angles.

The previous gray traffic-bearing waterproof membrane, while reasonably inconspicuous and inoffensive, certainly did not do justice to this space or to the quality and history of the building."

The architects chose to renovate the courtyard using Glacier Blue™ Devonian stone from Devonian Stone of New York, Inc. in Windsor, NY, because of its quality and high level of structural integrity. "We explored different suppliers in New York and Pennsylvania, but they displayed little interest," said Paplin. "They didn't have the attitude that they were ready to provide a superior product or attentive, intelligent service. [Robert Bellospirito from Devonian Stone] responded differently; quite the opposite actually. He was very enthusiastic right from the beginning, and he emphasized the quality of the stone and the consistency of color. Then he sent us some samples, which we loved. He completely fulfilled all our expectations."

According to Wender, they knew they were going to use stone all along. "Bluestone was the material that originally formed the sidewalks surrounding the building," he said. "It was a natural choice. I walked through the job with the client, and when we faced the building, we could see the existing Bluestone to the left and right. I recommended that the courtyard's sidewalks be finished in stone because that is what the original architect placed at the building's exterior. I felt it was best to carry the stone into the courtyard."

Three months later, Wender and his firm presented their findings to the Building's Board of Directors. After

The Devonian curbstones meet the granite pavers, which were all hand-carved and flame-finished.

discovering that the underlying steel structure was beginning to deteriorate, and would require a great deal of replacement and reinforcing, they suggested that the original finish material of concrete should be replaced by stone. "I came to this conclusion for two reasons," said Wender. "The original architect had used monolithic stones slabs at the exterior. Secondly, replacing the concrete would have required pouring a reinforced finish slab of a thickness that would have

Devonian stone was also used to clad the fountains within the courtyard.

According to Randy Huber of Cold Spring Granite, Inc., the Iridian granite used for the pavers was quarried in Isle, MN.

been prohibitive given the constraints of the project. Stone paving, sized in proportion to the existing Herculean slabs at the portal of the building, would be both more appropriate to the original architecture and technically accomplishable. "

Devonian Stone of New York, Inc. provided about 4,500 square feet of stone for the project — including paving stone and curbstones — all

flame-finished at the company's fabrication facility in Windsor, NY. Aside from supplying the stone for the Dakota's courtyard, Bellospirito also worked side-by-side with the contractor on the installation process, devising a method using a vacuum-operated jib crane to install each of the heavy stones, which measure from 3 ½ to 6 feet in size. According to the company, "the stone retains a high level of structural

integrity, providing cut tolerances of plus or minus ¼ to ¹⁄₁₆ inches to the finished product, allowing it to meet the most demanding architectural specifications."

According to Wender, the size of the stone slabs varies largely due to several factors. "First of all, I wanted to use very large slabs at the driveway to reflect the scale of the enormous slabs at the building's portal," he explained.

According to John Wender of Bartolone Wender Architects, the granite pavers are split on some faces, and cut on others. "They are split on four sides and sawn on two sides, with a flamed finished. We also chose them because they could be installed on a thinner bed," he explained.

A great deal of care was taken to ensure that all of the stonework would fit perfectly.

"Additionally, because the curb is formed by the stone slab itself, as opposed to a separate curbstone, I wanted the slabs forming the curb to be very large. The slabs then transition back to the perimeter of the building to a more easily manageable scale. The random sizes of the pattern reflect the patterning of the Bluestone on the building's exterior sidewalk."

"Landmarks required that we make the curbstones around the driveway in the center of the courtyard appear monolithic with the adjacent flagstones," said Paplin. "We wanted to use an L-shaped piece, but Bobby [Bellospirito] said not to because it would make the piece weak and subject to crack along the points of weakness. Plus, it required more labor to cut into an 'L,' so he told us to just keep it as a slab. What you see is what you get; it's a monumental monolithic 4- x 6-foot x 5-inch-thick piece."

According to Bellospirito, the pieces that Devonian Stone supplied were typically 2 or 5 inches thick, and they did run into a minor challenge when coordinating the stone at the site. "Space was limited," he said. "The contractor would send us a list of required pieces on a weekly basis for the following week. We would then fabricate them and get them down to him." He also experienced some difficulty due to the variety of the size of the pieces, which ranged from 3 x 3 feet to 5 x 8 x 9 inches in the south passageway.

During the mock-up process, the architects faced many challenges in regards to space. "It was difficult getting the entire system to work within the very narrow tolerances we had," said Paplin. "We only had 10 inches overall to do everything. After considering the paving thickness, the waterproofing and drainage system, a high enough curb and enough slope, we were left with little room for mistakes. It took two or three go-arounds of full-sized section details — measuring and then measuring again. It was gratifying in the end, and it all dropped into place beautifully. We even had an extra ⅛ inch when finished."

Stokdal Construction Corp. of Kingston, NY, completed the installation of the stone in about 10 months, with 22 workers on the job. According to Kaare Stokdal, the process was heavily involved and required the creation of new space before the stone could be implemented. "We had to remove the existing concrete and substructure, replace the steel, pour the concrete, redo the waterproofing and then install the Devonian stone and granite pavers," he said. The company used Portland cement and sand mortar, along with Jahn M110 pointing mortar distributed

Large blocks of Devonian Stone were cut at the plant in Windsor, NY.

by Cathedral Stone Products, Inc. from Hanover, MD.

In addition to Devonian stone the project also employed granite pavers. "We were going to use hexagon-shaped asphalt pavers like the ones used in Central Park and Riverside Park [in New York], but they were rejected for a combination of reasons," Paplin explained. "They wouldn't really fit into a courtyard like this." Instead, the architects chose to use granite pavers supplied by Cold Spring Granite Inc. of Cold Spring, MN.

Wender said that the natural decision was to use cobblestone, but because of the size of the project, this was difficult to do. "We wanted to choose something that looked like Belgium block, so we investigated granite pavers," he said. "Cold Spring has a good selection and a quality production record."

According to Wender, the granite pavers are split on some faces, and cut on others. He also said that the granite throughout the main part of the courtyard is 1 ½ inches thick, while the driveway pieces are 4 inches thick and lightly tumbled. "They are split on four sides and sawn on two sides, with a flame-faced finish. We also chose them because they could be installed on a thinner bed," he explained. "In the course of designing the paving pattern for the granite pavers at the driveway, I designed a herringbone pattern to reflect the guastivino tile ceiling vaults above, and help define the driveway as a special place. Subsequently, I discovered that the herringbone pattern is preferred in driveways because it is tighter and wears better than a stacked or running bond. Installation of the herringbone pattern with 4-inch pavers was very difficult, and the contractor should be commended for the hand sizing of each block that made this possible."

According to Randy Huber of Cold

A bridge saw was used to cut the stone slabs to the proper dimensions.

The process of flaming the stone pieces to the desired look was thorough and meticulous.

Spring Granite Inc., the company supplied 3,400 square feet of Iridian granite —quarried in Isle, MN — in various sizes, including 6 x 9 ½, 6 x 12, 14 x 14 and 3 ½ x 7 ½ inches. "We supplied the material as rectangular pieces," said Huber. "The contractor cut the perimeter pieces to fit. He also trimmed many of the field pieces in order to maintain exceptionally tight joints."

An interesting suggestion for the paver installation came from James Gainfort, who suggested that instead of using grout and mortar to set the stone, the crews should use Bluestone dust. "This is a somewhat unusual use of stone dust, but it was very appropriate for the project," said Paplin.

Wender also implemented stone planters, which he said were not an original element to the building. "I included a stone planter in the presentation of the landmark, and brought to attention that the tenants loved the original planter that was in place, and they agreed to it," he said. "It

is quite massive, and picks up the dimensions of the lantern fountains, which are the original cast iron ones — an historical element to the courtyard. We put a stone base on the lanterns and restored them. In the past, they were used to light up the basement, but now we use them to light up the courtyard at night to illuminate the Devonian stone and granite. We hid light bulbs inside them, and the light shines out through the windows."

Great care was taken to maintain a classical look despite the challenges of the site. "We were trying to strive to

keep to the spirit of the existing detailing, but had to tweak and invent in order to make the profiles work with the new heights and tolerances, and to replace profiles for which we no longer had direct evidence of the exact design," said Paplin. "Our overall objective was to create an articulate, coordinated whole that harmonizes the new with the original, and does not deny the present moment — the fact that this is 2004."

According to Wender, the tenants are "over the moon with excitement" about the renovation of the courtyard, which concluded this past September. ❑

### The Dakota Courtyard Renovation
### New York, NY

*Architects:* Bartolone Wender Architects, New York, NY; James R. Gainfort AIA Consulting Architects, New York, NY
*General Contactor/Stone Installer:* Stokdal Construction Corp., Kingston, NY
*Stone Suppliers:* Devonian Stone of New York, Inc., Windsor, NY (Glacier Blue™ sandstone); Cold Spring Granite, Inc., Cold Spring, MN (Iridian granite)
*Installation Products:* Cathedral Stone Products, Inc., Hanover, MD (Jahn M110 pointing mortar)

## Appendices

### APPENDIX A

EDWARD CLARK delivered the following paper at a meeting of the West End Association in 1879. It was published in the *Real Estate Record & Builders Guide* on 8 November 1879.

#### THE CITY OF THE FUTURE

If the original founders of the city of New York could have grasped the idea that in the course of years, and within a period not great when compared with the usual duration of great cities, the whole island would be surrounded by wharves and warehouses to accommodate the world's commerce, and its entire available area densely covered with buildings to meet the varied wants of a vast population, it is quite certain that the plans for public and private improvement would have been very different from those which have actually prevailed. To suit the convenience of the future city, the most important business of a public nature ought to be concentrated somewhere near the geographical centre of the island. Draw a line from the North to the East River, through Forty-second street and the intersection of that with the line of Broadway, would indicate and precisely, but somewhat nearly, the place where the Courts, the Exchange, the Custom House, the General Post Office, the large fraternal institutions, and all other business intimately connected with these, ought to be permanently located. The present existing arrangements are about as inconvenient as could have been devised. There is a daily congestion of the currents of humanity for several hours on the southerly point of the island which is painful to experience or contemplate, and a corresponding depletion toward the evening. The elevated railways, to a certain degree alleviate this evil, but never can cure it. The struggle of opposing interests is always going on, and cannot be expected to cease until the city is finally completed. Persons who are not yet old can remember when the little triangle called Hanover square, south of the present Custom House was considered the cluster seat of the greatest trade in the city, and many can recall the time when it would have been thought absurd to try to establish a wholesale business anywhere west of Broadway. Things look differently now, and there is no reason to suppose great changes will cease to be made. Wall street still gallantly holds its own, but who can tell when or how soon the money changers and their satellites will be compelled to seek other temples.

In our city of the future it seems to me, no single lot on the surface of the island can properly or profitably be spared for a small or inferior building. It is the duty, and ought to be considered a great privilege of the property owners, of the present time, to exercise a judicious foresight as to the manner in which their lots shall be improved and to see to it that buildings erected hereafter shall be permanent in their character.

Looking out from my office window across Union Square I see two very prominent edifices for business purposes – they are the third series of buildings erected on the same sites within a few years – and the most conspicuous and costly private residence in the city stands on the spot where a large and handsome brown stone house was demolished to give it room. The tearing down process has been already carried on to an enormous extent, and there are yet very large districts already built over, where the buildings must be razed to the ground to give place to better. Probably this mushroom-style of building was inevitable during the former period of ignorance and uncertainty. But hereafter there will be no excuse for such improvident and wasteful building. Considering what has been done, it is not difficult to forecast the future, and the building which is done now can be and ought be such as will be appropriate to the city a hundred years hence.

It is fortunate for those interested in this Association that building west of Central Park and above Fifty-ninth street has been so significantly retarded. There is but little except the shanties that requires to be torn down.

I believe some diverse opinions have been expressed in regard to the character of the buildings which ought to be erected on the space between the westerly side of the Central Park and the Hudson River. Some have thought the most profitable course would be to erect small and cheap houses for persons of moderate means. These gentlemen entertain a sincere belief that the wealth and magnificence of New York has exhausted, or will exhaust itself upon Fifth and Madison avenues. But I presume most of the members of this association have a firm belief that the attractive combination of the Central, Riverside and Morningside parks, and the admirable conformation of the land between them, will give this district a sure and distinguished pre-eminence. Our newspaper paragraphists are very fond of speaking of the merchant princes of New York, and perhaps our wealthy citizens are not averse to being thus designated. No doubt it is true that there are many persons in New York whose incomes are princely in amount, but princes ought to live in palaces, and where are they? To use the idea and language of Gen. Vièle, "few persons have thought of constructing anything more than three-quarters of a house." Gentlemen who have visited Genoa and Venice will remember the palaces which princes who were merchants in former times built in those cities: and from that may form some idea of what merchants who wish to be like princes may hereafter do in the way of construction in New York, particularly if they select the West Side plateau as the scene of their munificence.

The practical question presents itself – how ought the West Side to be improved? We will agree, I think, that it should be built so as to accommodate a great number of families, some splendidly, many elegantly, and all comfortably. That the architecture should be ornate, solid and permanent, and that the principle of economic combination should be employed to the greatest possible extent.

Thus far in the better parts of the city the general plan has been to build single houses, each owner of a lot exercising his own taste, or displaying the want of it, without reference to the wishes of his neighbors, and without any particular regard to the effect of his work upon the appearance of the city.

It is to be hoped that a new era in building is about to commence, in which intelligent combined effort will produce novel and splendid results. I will say that for myself, I am in favor of apartment houses for the improvement of the West Side plateau. The general plan of apartment houses, or French flats, has been considerably employed in New York, and from the first has met with distinguished favor. Most of them, thus far, have been cheaply built to accommodate people of very limited means. Some few have been very thoroughly and elegantly constructed, with a view to being occupied by small families who can afford to expend from five to ten thousand dollars a year. The advantages and economies of these superior dwellings have been so evident that they have always been eagerly taken by excellent tenants as soon as ready for occupancy. The economy will be understood when I state, as probably others can, that I have paid at a leading hotel in New York, for seven or eight consecutive months, at the rate of seven thousand dollars a year for the rent of two small rooms, and that I am able now to rent to others suites of nine rooms, finished in the best possible way, and adopted to all the requirements of elegant housekeeping for fifteen hundred dollars a year. There are but few persons who are princely enough to wish to occupy an entire palace, and possibly most of those who are best able to do it, would be most unwilling to take upon themselves the inevitable worry and trouble: but I believe there are many who would like to occupy a portion of a great building, which would be more perfect in its arrangements than any palace in Europe, unless it would be one of very recent construction. For the principal streets and avenues of the West Side plateau, I should be disposed to advocate the construction of apartment houses, with suites of rooms varying in size and number so as to be suited to the uses of families having the ability to expend from five thousand to fifty thousand dollars or over a year. There is hardly any limit to the rate of expenditure and style of social splendor, to which the apartment house might not easily be adapted, but whatever the scale might be, it is quite certain that for a given amount of money a vastly greater amount of convenience, comfort and display might be secured. There is a considerable class, and such as would be especially desirable on the West Side, who have houses out of the city in which they wish to reside the greater part of the year. To all these the advantages of an apartment in town, into which they could come, and out of which they could go, at any time, are very obvious. But the comparative advantages of apartment houses over single dwellings, though many, I have no time to discuss now.

The question arises – how are these buildings to be erected, and who are to pay for them? In other cities such houses are built, and certainly the ability exists to construct them here. The first and main point is to establish the necessity for them. The very best and most economical way to prosecute a grand scheme of improvement would perhaps be something like this:

Suppose a whole block on the West Side to have no buildings on it, and the lots to be owned by twenty difference persons, in different proportions. Suppose the time to have arrived when most of these owners are of the opinion that the block should be built upon. Evidently, it is for the interest of all to have their property improved in the best way, and so as to secure the greatest profit. By combining together, employing a single architect and building upon the entire block as one enterprise, the work could be done with much greater economy than by any individual effort, and a splendid result could be attained. As the owners of some of these lots would be much more wealthy than others, those least able to bear the expense of building ought to be able to borrow from the richer as much money as would be required, and at a low rate of interest, as the security would be perfect. When such a building should be completed, it might be divided by commissioners, expert in the business, in accordance with the ownership of the land, and the cost of building might be equitably apportioned in the same way. Thus all parties would be benefited, the wealthier owners by preventing injury to their property by the erection of inferior buildings and the poorer ones by sharing in the advantages of a great capital at moderate interest. The city would gain in the splendid character of the improvements. This is only a suggestion of a plan, but I feel confident it might be elaborated and put into successful execution.

It may be objected, perhaps, that in this outlined scheme no provision has been made for the laboring population. There is the highest authority for believing that the poor will always be with us, but it does not follow that the poor will necessarily occupy any of the West Side plateau. Indeed, I think we should agree that the very poor would be sufficiently with us if they should fix their habitations in New Jersey or on Long Island. But to accommodate the industrious and meritorious working people, the same plans should be pursued substantially as in providing dwellings for the rich.

The model dwelling for the poor man should occupy a space, not 25 by 100 feet, but an entire block. It should be quite plain, but solid and substantial in every part. The rooms for each family should be of moderate size and few in number, but every room should have good air and light. Water should be supplied to each apartment or suite of rooms, and they should be heated by steam. The building should be made quite safe as to fire, and a passenger elevator should convey the tenants up and down. All this and more could be furnished to the laboring population, as cheaply as the miserable rooms in tenement houses which they are obliged to occupy now. I suppose the owners of such a model tenement house ought to be, and would be, satisfied with 5 per cent upon the investment, over and above all expenses. In such a case cheapness and very superior accommodations would naturally and easily follow from the vast extent of the enterprise, and the greatly increased number of families who would thus be furnished with homes.

The advantages, in a sanitary point of view, of the plans for building, which have been faintly suggested, would be greater than can well be estimated, and it would be easy, as to such dwellings, to exercise a most rigid supervision and effective police.

Probably some judicious legislation might be advisable to aid the formation of combined building associations; but even under the present general laws I believe, with a reasonable and proper feeling among the owners and adjacent lots, whatever is needful might be done to the great mutual advantage of all concerned.

# APPENDIX B

THE FOLLOWING article about the then-unnamed Van Corlear appeared in the 4 April 1878 issue of the *American Architect and Building News.*

## A NEW APARTMENT HOUSE DESIGN

Mr. HENRY J. HARDENBERGH, architect, has in hand an apartment house, which is to stand upon Seventh Avenue, between Fifty-fifth and Fifty-sixth streets, west side. With a frontage of 200 feet upon the avenue, and a depth of 100 feet upon either of the streets, an opportunity is given for a complete work, while the several angles and the chance given for distant views call for care in design. There are many points in which Mr. Hardenbergh has left the traditions, which have thus far controlled the designing of this class of buildings in New York. The Hardenbergh flat is the first apartment house yet built which has a semblance of the Queen Anne features in it. They are kept under control. There is no riotous brickwork or exuberant trivialities of form and outline, but a general flavor of the new favorite in the great exterior. The building is really a double one, the main entrances being on the side streets, and each entrance leading to three flats, with six stories in all ; this gives a total of thirty-six suites of apartments for the whole block. A feature of the plan is the absence of air shafts or light-wells, those chimney-like excavations which are so often thrust down into masses of structure, with the fond belief that they furnish all in the way of light and air which any ordinary dwelling room should require. In place of these deceptive and expensive little air funnels, the plan has been so arranged as to throw the entire sum of these air ducts into one great area, 90 x 35 feet; and instead of carrying his construction entirely above this, an artery is left open to the west, leading into the centre of the lines of dwellings beyond, and acting as a feeder to what might otherwise become the stagnant mass of air in the area. This whole question of airshafts would repay a few careful observations and experiments, to determine exactly what motions of air do actually take place, and under what conditions the mass of atmosphere remains strictly stagnant. With the ample space at his command, Mr. Hardenbergh has been enabled to make a real suite of apartments, placed in that juxtaposition which their uses and importance demand. Instead of being strung along a passage, like cells on a corridor, the rooms are grouped, the social or guest room about an ante-room or lobby, while the family or private rooms are placed in more retired situations. There are elevators and lifts, and the usual drying and servants' rooms in the seventh story, which does not show from the street. There will not be stores at present upon the first floor, though the construction is such that a change could easily be effected. The materials of the exterior will be Philadelphia brick and Nova Scotia stone, the latter freely used. There is also a liberal use of terra-cotta panels at various points; iron, except in the fireproof construction, has been entirely avoided, and from foundation stone to cornice the construction is devoid of all sham and pretense. The whole, finished in a thoroughly first-class manner, by percentage or day's work, will cost about $300,000. Edward Clark, the president of the Singer Manufacturing Company, is the owner, and so far no name has been selected for the structure.

## APPENDIX C

A LTHOUGH the following article appeared in the 4 April 1878 issue of the *Real Estate Record and Building News,* the same issue date as the prior article, it evidently had been written later (or at least had later information), as the new building had been named according to this article. This article also includes the earliest known projection of what was to become the Dakota, as well as the row of houses on West 73rd Street and the small apartment house on the southwest corner of 73rd Street and Ninth Avenue (as Columbus Avenue was then called). There is also a projection for a large French-style apartment house on the corner of Eighth Avenue and 74th Street, whose plans are said to have already been completed, but that project was never built.

### THE VAN CORLEAR

I t is well that among the crop of apartment houses that has sprung up in modern New York during the past five years there is now to be found at least one which helps to remind us of our own history, brief though it be. The Dutch of New Amsterdam deserve to be remembered in these days for active thrift, and the example here placed before us by the owner of this vast apartment house is well worthy of imitation. This is not a country of monuments, nor an age of poetry, and our practical modern houses, constructed on a large scale, if they must at all perpetuate the memory of a person or an event, should serve at least as monuments that keep alive a history of which we may well be proud, without endeavoring to blazon constantly before our eyes names and titles that are foreign to this soil and unsympathetic in the memories they recall.

This building fronting the entire block on Seventh avenue, from Fifty-fifth to Fifty-sixth street, shows the progress we are making even in the construction of apartment houses. It is the only one, in fact, or rather the first which has a courtyard worthy of the name and such as the Parisians understand it. True, there is not yet the *porte cochère,* but nevertheless, all the other appurtenances are there, and the court itself extends over 3,500 square feet and an entrance is provided for wagons that can find access to the place by a roadway especially constructed for that purpose. A lady recently returned from Paris after having looked everywhere for a suite of apartments congenial to her tastes secured them at last in the Van Corlear, expressing her astonishment at the progress made in this respect by our builders during the past five years.

Fronting, as already stated, the Seventh avenue, this apartment house extends one hundred feet on each side street, where the two main entrances are, leaving an entire unbroken line along the avenue. If we should find any fault at all, and desire to be hypercritical, it is in this unbroken barrack-looking line along the avenue that we dislike. As it is, the front lower story looks somewhat monotonous, and the eye seeks for relief in vain along the two hundred feet of massive-straight lines that extend from block to block. This, however, is a matter of taste, and as the architect, no doubt, will say against the established rules of design. It is just because this is a fact that we should like to have seen Mr. Hardenbergh try the innovation. The structure rises to immense proportions with its six stories and attic of Philadelphia brick, but there the eye is greatly relieved by the terra cotta and other trimmings that ornament this vast front.

Coming back to the court-yard, which contains a most welcome fountain, we find that the entrance above alluded to is on the west side, and a paved passage way connects this court with the street, the yard proper being laid with an asphalt pavement. It is from this court that the practical utility of the Van Corlear can best be contemplated. Each of the six stories of the building contains six suites of rooms, and each suite has at least nine, and a few have ten rooms. Not a single dark room has been found among those thirty-six suites of apartments, either the room has a window on the avenue or side street or the vast court-yard.

No less than seven elevators have been furnished by the Otis Brothers for this structure. Of these, two are for passengers on either street and five so-called lifts, for the hoisting of furniture and supplies. Each suite has a lobby opening on the main hall and an ante-room in addition. The principal rooms are in all cases near the entrance and the kitchens so disposed as to be quite unobtrusive. Ample coal and wine cellars have been provided and a separate drying room for each suite will be found in the attic.

Brick walls separate each suite of rooms and the various partition walls are of strong, fire proof material. There is one very great advantage to be found in the Van Corlear and that is no stores are connected with it. It is a private dwelling house throughout and as such far more eligible than those would-be fashionable apartment houses, which look more like huge markets than private dwellings.

That a building of this description is eagerly wanted in New York is evidenced by the fact that though the Van Corlear will not be ready for occupancy until September 1st nearly all the suites have been disposed of to excellent tenants at a rental ranging from $1,000 to $1,500. The owner is Mr. Edward Clark, President of the Singer Manufacturing Company, who has expended $300,000 on the construction of the building. The architect is Mr. H. J. Hardenbergh, of 111 Broadway, who claims his production as a pure Renaissance with considerable of the Queen Anne features about it.

A host of workingmen have been employed all by day's work, in bringing this vast structure to its actual completion. It was last year that Mr. John D. Crimmins first began to excavate the rock, when shortly after the foundations were laid by Mr. John Banta, assisted by his foreman, Washington Cooper, who had subsequently charge of all the mason work. The Philadelphia brick, hard brick, Croton fronts, cement, hair and lime came from the old house of Rove & Denman. The ordinary carpenter work has been furnished by John L. Hamilton, of West Twenty-seventh street, but all the doors, sashes, trimmings, etc., have been made at the Singer Manufacturing shop, at South Bend, Ind., where they have large cabinet works. Still, the hallway trimmings, which required considerable skill, were made by the Pottier & Stymus Manufacturing Company. The stairs are all of iron and marble, the fine iron work being done by Poulson & Eger, of South Brooklyn, and the marble by A. L. Fouchere, of Broadway and Thirty-fourth street. Fisher & Bird have supplied the marble mantels and the whole of the marble trimmings to the wooden mantels throughout the building, and Pottier & Stymus the wooden. Artistic grates, feeders and fire places in brass, nickel and bronze were furnished by W. H. Jackson & Co., Seventeenth street and Union square. The iron for the servants' staircases and the work connected therewith, also all the ornamental iron railing, window guard, grating, iron doors for dumb waiters, lattice dates under the stoop, iron balconies and iron roof has been furnished by G. R. Jackson's Sons, of Centre street, and all the fire proof articles by the Fire-Proof Building Company. All the fire-proof partitions in the building, except the brick walls, were manufactured and erected by Gustavus Isaacs, the well-known proprietor of the Empire Plaster Mills, Bethune street. The English tiles in the hall have been supplied by Aspinwall & Son. All the halls, twelve in number (except the lower hall), thirty vestibules and thirty-five small landings were tiled with the beautiful Spanish mosaic floor tiles purchased from John Chadwick, 49 Broadway.

The plumbing, which the owner claims is better than is to be found in any apartment house, was attended to by Timothy Brien, of Bleecker street. The iron stoneware sewer pipe for this building was furnished by G. W. Rader & Co., 611 West Fifty-first street. Messrs Mitchell & Vance supplying all the gas fixtures. Messrs James & Kirkland supplied the Beebe ranges; Usal Cory, of Water street, furnished the numerous elevated oven ranges, while the Angell & Blake Manufacturing Company had charge of the steam heating apparatus. All the mirrors throughout the building came from Semon Bache & Co., in Duane street. The knobs, locks and hinges, as well as other bronze work were from special designs and specially adapted for this building, from the Hopkins & Dickinson Manufacturing Co., the bell works being under the special charge of David Murray's Sons, 627 Sixth avenue.

Great praise is due for the manner in which Schillinger has laid the pavement in the court-yard. The sidewalk was also laid and fountain erected by Mr. Schillinger, while James Gillis, as the foot of Fifteenth street, had charge of the stone work. The terra cotta ornaments have all been purchased from the Perth Amboy Terra Cotta Works, 170 Broadway, and the blue stone from A. S. Dickinson. As to roofing, the credit of the metal work belongs to Edward Crommelin, of Washington street, and the roofing proper to Tobias New, of John street.

OTHER IMPROVEMENT BY THE SAME OWNER: The value of the above improvements to this section of the city will be better appreciated when it becomes generally known that Mr. Clark, the owner of the Van Corlear, is actively at work now in improving other parcels, which he owns, on the extreme west side. The work begun by him cannot fail to give an impetus to building in that excellent section, which, unfortunately, has been neglected too long. On the north side of Seventy-third street, west of Ninth avenue, Mr. Clark is now building twenty-five private houses and one corner apartment house, with store underneath, facing on Ninth avenue; of these private houses, nine will be four stories high and sixteen three-story. They have thus far progressed in sharp, workmanlike style, the beams for the parlor floor being just put in. All of these houses will be first class, of brick and sandstone, and will be provided with all modern improvements. The corner 'flats" will be thirty feet wide by ninety-six feet deep, and the store will be an ornament to the avenue. The entrance to the flat, however, will be on Seventy-third street, quite distinct from the store, which the private houses on the street will have nothing in common, nor any connection whatever with the so-called apartment house on the corner.

The erection of the Van Corlear has given Mr. Clark a true insight into the actual requirements of our city. As already stated, the various suites in that building had not, by any means reached completion when there at once arose a pressing demand for them, resulting in their all being taken by well-to-do tenants at satisfactory rentals before even the mechanics could see the end of their labors. Taking advantage of the experience thus gathered, Mr. Clark proposes to erect on the southwest corner of Seventy-fourth street and Eighth Avenue, a first class apartment house, strictly in accordance with the French style. The rooms and suites will be considerably larger than those on Seventh avenue, and their entire construction will be with the single aim of furnishing persons of a better class with eligible domiciles at a comparatively low rental. Each tier of apartments will be provided with an independent staircase. There will also be a large court in the centre, with two *porte cochère* entrances, one on Eighth avenue and one on Seventy-fourth street. The plans for this building, which will be six or seven stories high, have been fully completed by Mr. Hardenbergh the architect, but it is not believed that Mr. Clark will begin building operations there till next spring. We can say this much, however, that according to the designs it will be the most thorough French apartment house in the city.

In addition to the above, Mr. Clark owns the plot of ground on the Eighth avenue, with 375 feet on Seventy-second street, and the same on Seventy-third street. This locality is close to the Seventy-second street entrance to the Central Park and bound to be before long the most frequented spot in the city. It is indeed difficult to tell for an investor what class of building will be the most remunerative there, but it strikes us that Mr. Clark's idea to erect a grand hotel on this spot will everywhere be hailed with applause. He justly thinks that the time is not far off when New York will require in that locality as colossal a hotel as the Grand Hotel, of Paris, and no better site could possibly be found for such an enterprise as this charming neighborhood. The plans for this mammoth hotel have, however, not as yet been perfected. Whenever they are, we shall recur to this enterprise again.

# APPENDIX D

PERHAPS picking up the topic from the above two articles in competing periodicals, in its 20 April 1878 issue the *Real Estate Record & Builders' Guide* published the following article

## MR. CLARK'S MAMMOTH APARTMENT HOUSE.

The line of the Seventh avenue, for some reason or other has heretofore not been a very popular locality for important improvements, but when prominent property owners, like Mr. Clark, President of the Singer Manufacturing Company have the foresight of taking advantage of the present low prices of material to erect handsome buildings there, the dark cloud that has so long, and without any adequate reason, hung over that avenue will soon be dispelled. The improvement on which Mr. Clark has set his mind is not by any means a trivial one, and when the work is completed he will have the satisfaction of owning the most extensive apartment house in New York.

The entire block, between Fifty-fifth and Fifty-sixth streets, swarms now with workingmen, laying the foundation for an as yet unchristened apartment house that will have a frontage of two hundred feet on the avenue and one hundred feet on each of the side streets. The building which is to be erected in the Queen Anne style, will have no stores on the lower floor, and will be six stories high, each story to contain six suites of apartments, making thirty six suites in all.

The main and distinguishing feature of the plans prepared for this building by Mr. H. J. Hardenbergh, architect, of 111 Broadway, is that in true French style, there will be a large court in the centre measuring 35x126 feet, with an outlet on the block, so that each suite of rooms will have not only a good outlook on the street but also on the court, which is to be embellished with attractive flower beds. This great advantage of a court—that is to be a court, indeed—shows that our architects, if only sufficient room is given them, are slowly coming up to the true French Idea of apartment houses, so that all the service for the building can come through this court leaving the main entrances for the exclusive use of visitors. These main entrances are to be on the side streets, leaving the entire Seventh avenue front in an unbroken line free to represent, what it really will be, an imposing structure. One half of the block, however, will be the exact counterpart of the other, the whole forming together such a gigantic edifice as Gothamite eyes have not heretofore rested upon, except when contemplating either the Windsor or Fifth avenue hotels.

The excavations for this mammoth apartment house have been completed by the contractor, John D. Crimmins, with wonderful expedition. The rock there laid very uneven, which necessitated the contractors to go in deeper and make a sort of pocket in the earth near Fifty-sixth street. He had to blast a great deal with the steam drill, and still his work was concluded before the time called for by the contract.

His place has now been taken by Mr. John Banta, master builder, of 294 West Fourth street, who has charge of the entire mason work, and now has an army of men on the ground all actively engaged in laying the four-foot foundation wall, every inch of which, so to speak, is being carefully looked after by Mr. Cooper. Mr. Banta's experienced foreman. The work is done by the day and is progressing satisfactorily to the owner and architect. The front is to be of Philadelphia brick, to be furnished, by Rowe & Denman, with Nova Scotia stone, and also terra cotta trimmings. Mr. James Gillis, foot of West Fiftieth Street, will furnish this Nova Scotia stone and also do the cutting, while the terra cotta, of which we have seen some fine specimens, will probably be obtained from Hull & Sons, in Perth Amboy, for whom Mr. Frank, in Murray street, is the general agent. The latter contract, has, however, not yet been concluded and may still be considered open for the competition of others.

As this building is to be entirely fireproof it will be of interest to the various firms interested in this particular line to be informed that the contract for this work has not yet been awarded, and will not be for a week or ten days. The delivery of the iron beams has been separately arranged for with a Pennsylvania firm, which took the contract at a very low figure, but so far as the actual fireproof material is concerned the door for competition for this vast building stands wide open. Both Mr. Schillinger's and Mr. Beckwith's claims will be duly considered, also Lyons & Bunn, who we understand, propose to call the architect's attention to their excellent composition.

The ordinary carpenter work, such as pine wood flooring and other ordinary matters pertaining thereto, will be entrusted to Mr. John L. Hamilton, of 150 West Twenty-seventh street, who bears an excellent reputation in the trade, but all the hard wood and trimmings will be attended to at the works of the Singer Manufacturing Company and will receive special care and supervision from Mr. Hamilton.

In order to make the building thoroughly fire proof the two main stair-cases will be of iron. For this iron work, as well as other, estimates have already been received from the Cornell's, and also from the Excelsior foundry of G. R. Jackson's Sons, 201 Centre street. Mr. Burnett is also competing for this contract, which will also be decided now in a very few days.

The two passenger elevators required for this buildings will be supplied by the firm of Wm. E. Hale & Co.

As the rooms will all be nicely grouped, leaving the family and private apartments in a more retired part of each suite, the question of ventilation and steam heating becomes a very important one for this building. The contracts for steam heating, not yet given out, are open for competition. Messrs. Angell & Blake, Messrs. Gillis & Geoghegan, and W. H. Warner, of Leonard street, being the principal competitors.

There will be a flat and a peaked roof on the building, the former to be covered with slate, the flat roof with cement and gravel.

The entire building will, when completed, not cost over $300,000, a small sum considering the vast ground it covers but everything will be furnished in first class style and the architect and builder unite in a desire to erect a building that will not only be satisfactory and remunerative to the owner, but ornamental to the City of New York.

# APPENDIX E

On 3 June 1882, while the Dakota was approaching the midpoint in its construction, the *Real Estate Record & Guide* published this article:

## VAST APARTMENT HOUSES.

Unless all the indications are deceptive, before five years are over New York will have the largest and best appointed apartment houses in the world. Every week some new plan is filed, and the last design has some attractive novelty not thought of when these great establishments were first erected. In one of the projected Madison avenue Paris flats there is to be a garden on the top; another proposes to have a Turkish or Russian bath for the use of its inmates. Mr. José F. de Navarro's series of houses on Fifty-ninth street will contain many novel features, as will also Mr. Clark's "Dakota" on Eighth avenue and Seventy-second street. The most magnificent scheme of all, however, is that of Mr. W. H. Post. His project is not yet in a shape to present in all its details to the public, but enough is known to settle the fact that it will be the most ambitious structure of the kind in the world. It is to be located near the Central Park, probably on the West Side, and will cover an entire block. There will be two hundred suites of rooms, each occupying on an average 25x85 feet space. It is understood that the Astor estate is interested in this great scheme, which is to be something more than a mere place of residence, for the projectors have in mind certain co-operative features. It is intended to supply certain articles of food for daily use at wholesale prices. Coal will be bought by the boat load and distributed, dressed meat or cattle will be contracted for at wholesale rates, and every effort will be made to furnish needed supplies at a minimum cost, the object being to abolish the corner grocery man, and save to householders the profits they now pay out to the minor stores.

There is a report in circulation that Mr. James Gordon Bennett intends to erect the finest hotel in the world upon a portion, if not all the block bounded by Fifth and Madison avenues, Thirty-eighth and Thirty-ninth streets. As the buildings on the ground are too valuable to be removed, they are to be utilized in a sort of composite structure, and thus will be afforded a great variety of apartments for the guests of the hotel, the lessees of which will be the gentlemen who now have charge of the Brevoort House. This last hotel, by the way, will probably be abandoned, and the building put to some other use, as it is out of the region travelers care to patronize; it may indeed be made into an apartment house. It is known that Mr. Bennett has acquired some adjoining property to his house on Fifth avenue. As much as two years ago he contemplated erecting an apartment house. It may be that the large payment to his sister, in settlement of the estate, may interfere with his building designs. Rich as he is, the raising of nearly $700,000 in cash must be somewhat of a strain upon him.

The demand for suites of rooms in apartment houses is far in excess of the supply. It is understood that, although far from completion, the Dakota, belonging to Mr. Clark, on Eighth avenue, is bespoken to the extent of two-thirds of its accommodations. Quite a number of Mr. Navarro's apartments are also already engaged. Among the immense structures which have been filed at the Building Department since the first of January are the following. A perusal of this list will give our readers some idea of the vastness of the buildings, and the large sums of money to be laid out in their construction. It will be seen that if these buildings multiply, New York will soon contain more palaces than all the capitals of Europe.

Northeast corner Broadway and Sixty-second street, eight-story, 116.2x139.11x100.5x87.1. Owner. Abraham Benson. Cost, $500,000.

Southwest corner Park avenue and Sixty-second street, nine story brick and brown stone, Byzantine style, 100.5x85. Owner, William Van Antwerp. Cost, $175.000. Architect, W. H. Cauvet.

North side of Seventy-second street, 100 feet east of the Boulevard, eight-story brick and brown stone, Venetian style, 90x90. Owner, William V. A. Mulhallon. Architect. W. H. Cauvet. Cost, $125,000.

Southwest corner Seventh avenue and Fifty-seventh street, seven-story, commenced about fifteen months ago by William F. Croft. Now owned and being erected by William Noble. Cost, $250,000.

Fifth avenue and Twenty-eighth street, southeast corner, 100x125. Owners, Stock Company. Architects, Hubert Pirsson & Co. Cost, including the ground, $1,000,000.

North side Seventy-second street, 250 feet west of Third avenue, seven-story brick and Dorchester stone, 39.6x93. Owner, William Noble. Architect, Geo. W. DaCunha. Cost, $75,000.

Northwest corner Ninth avenue and Seventy-eighth street, eight-story brick and terra cotta, 102x100. Owner, James O'Friel. Architect, E. Gruwé. Cost, $250,000.

Northeast corner Madison avenue and Thirtieth street, ten-story brick, 91.6x110. Owners, G. P. Lowrey et al. Architects, Hubert Pirsson & Co. Cost, $300,000.

Fifty-seventh street, north side, 75 feet east of Sixth avenue, seven-story brown stone, 69.5x90. Owner, Jacob B. Tallman. Architect, H. J. Dudley. Cost, $200,000.

North side Seventy-sixth street, 185 feet east of Madison avenue, 60x92, seven-story brownstone. Owner, Frederick Aldhous. Cost, $90,000.

Northeast corner Fifth avenue and Twenty-eighth street, nine-story brick and brown stone, 75x150. Owner. Stock Company. Architects, Hubert Pirsson & Co. Cost, $850,000.

Nos. 40 and 42 East Twenty-fifth street, six-story brick and terra cotta, 50x86.8. Owners, The Barrington Association. Architect, Carl Pfeiffer. Cost, $100,000.

Northwest corner of Eighth avenue and Forty-sixth street, two five-story brick, one 85x73, the other 40x83, to cost respectively $120,000 and $60,000. Owner, John Jacob Astor. Architect, Thomas Stent.

Southwest corner of Broadway and Fifty-fourth street, seven-story, 52x71.5x75.5. Owner, Victor B Dispurris. Architect, A. B. Ogden.

Nos. 12 and 14 West Eighteenth street, six-story brick and brown stone, 58 x half the block. Owner, a stock company. Architect, August Hatfield: cost, $120,000.

Northwest corner of Eighth avenue and Sixty-second street, nine-story brick and stone, 100x115. Owner, a co-operative association. Architect, Carl Pfeiffer; cost, $250,000.

By far the most extensive improvement in the shape of apartment houses is the proposed erection, by Mr. José F. De Navarro, of ten mammoth houses on the plot of ground between Fifty-eighth and Fifty-ninth streets, and east of Seventh avenue. These houses will all be nine stories high and the material to be used is granite, brown stone, Ohio stone and Milwaukee and Philadelphia brick. They will be in the Moorish style of architecture, and it is estimated that the total cost of construction will be $3,000,000. Contracts have just been signed for the construction of the four houses nearest to Seventh avenue and which are to be known as the Lisbon, Madrid, Cordova and Barcelona. These houses are to be divided by passageways 25 feet wide, above which there will be easy means of access, on every floor, from one house to the other in case of any sudden conflagration. The halls and stairways will all be lined with enameled brick, which does away with the use of laths, plastering, etc. Mr. R. Deeves has been appointed general superintendent and work was commenced on these four houses on June 1st, and it is confidently stated that they will be completed in sixteen months from that day. Out of the fifty-two apartments, all have been sold but thirteen. About August let work will be commenced on four more of these houses, and the erection of the remaining six houses will be pushed as soon as possible. The architects are Messrs. Hubert, Pirsson & Co., and the agents, Messrs. Lespinasse & Friedman.

In this connection we may mention that Mr. Edward Clark's family hotel, the Dakota, will be completed by next spring at a cost of nearly $1,500,000. It is eight stories high, built of brick and Dorchester stone and covers the entire front on Eighth avenue from Seventy-second to Seventy-thirdstreet, 204.4x200. Architect, H. J. Hardenbergh.

# APPENDIX F

THE 21 SEPTEMBER 1889 EDITION of the *Real Estate Record & Guide* reported on the first of the new apartment hotels that were built in emulation of the successful Dakota and which later were taken down for their namesake apartment houses that now exist.

## THE HOTEL BERESFORD.

This fine building, an illustration of which is presented herewith, is an example of the new mode of living due to the desire to avoid the cares of housekeeping. It is the first of its kind ever built west of the Central Park, and its success, already assured, opens up a new vista to the builder and capitalist. The Beresford is not a hotel in the usual acceptation of the word. It is what is in future to be known as an "apartment hotel." That is, it is comprised of a number of suites for families and bachelors, which they occupy just as though they lived in an apartment house like the Dakota, the Osborne, the Rutland, or any other first-class flat. But it differs from them in this respect, that no cooking is done in any of the suites, as everyone eats in a large dining-room, the meals of which are cooked, served and supplied by the owner and manager of the building. There are no kitchens or culinary appliances in any of the suites, for the simple reason that they are unnecessary. All one requires to do is to eat, drink, sleep and pay one's check when it becomes due, the cares of house-keeping being shouldered upon the proprietor of the hotel. Ladies who have for years been breaking their hearts over their troubles with servants will no doubt welcome with open arms the new era of apartment hotels which has just dawned upon us.

The Hotel Beresford is situated on the northwest corner of Central Park West and 81st street within one block of the "L" station. It has an imposing exterior and its windows overlook Manhattan square on the one side and Central Park on the other, views which will be uninterrupted as long as the building stands. It contains thirty-four suites of apartments, some two-thirds of which have already been rented, although the building will not be ready for occupancy until October 1st. The rents of these suites range from $1,200 to $1,800 each, according to their size and location. They contain four rooms, with a bathroom and all other conveniences, while there is steam heat throughout. There are several bachelor apartments, which are considerably lower in price. The rents include chamber and waiting service, like any large hotel. Every suite enters upon a wide hallway, and the elevators bring the upper floors practically within as easy access as the lower floors. The dining-room is a superb room on the seventh floor. It is delightfully located, as it places the guests, while they are taking their meals, in full view of Central and Manhattan Parks, the Museums of Art and Natural History and other objects. To dine under such conditions must surely aid both appetite and digestion. In order to attract tenants and make them feel perfectly content to remain in their quarters the proprietor appears to have adopted a wise plan. He has cut down the cost of meals to as low a sum as is consistent with good food and service, the figure being understood to be $7 per capita weekly. This makes life in an apartment hotel not only easy, but comparatively inexpensive.

The entrance to the building is quite handsome and spacious, the hallway being 18 feet wide. There are two elevators to conduct tenants to their different suites of rooms, and the apartments are of an attractive character, all the improvements being introduced. The owner and manager, Mr. Alva S. Walker, is the same gentleman who built the Winthrop on 7th avenue and 125th street, an apartment hotel which has been remarkably successful.

The ground on which the Beresford stands has, by the way, quite a little history. It is one of the choicest and most costly on the west side of the city, and was formerly owned by José F. de Navarro. The latter, indeed, once filed plans for the erection of a grand fireproof apartment building on the site, but owing to financial complications in which he became involved, due to underestimating the cost of the Central Park apartment houses, he mortgaged this and other properties to secure advances, and the mortgagee, Jas. J McComb, the well-known millionaire, subsequently acquired the property under foreclosure proceedings. He then sold it to John D. Crimmins, who, in his turn, sold it to Mr. Walker, the present owner. The latter owns a plot of four lots adjoining the Hotel Beresford, on the southwest corner of 82nd street and Central Park West. These he proposes to turn into a small park, and he has in contemplation the laying out of two tennis courts in the centre, with seats around, for the use of the guests in the hotel. This idea, if carried out, will prove an attractive feature.

The Beresford is probably only the beginning of an era of apartment hotel building on the west side. The advantages of such a mode of living as these buildings afford will in future attract hundreds of families to whom the inconvenience and expenses of housekeeping have become a burden.

# APPENDIX G

THE EDITION of the *Real Estate Record and Builders Guide* for 28 September 1889 gave expanded coverage to one aspect of the increased West Side building activity.

## THE APARTMENT HOTEL.

For some time a new departure in the way of building has been taking place in this city which has only been made possible in consequence of the exceptional conditions of living in the metropolis. This departure is a new one and yet it is old. It is nothing more or less that the erection of hotels on the family plan of a simpler and less expensive character than the old ones, yet with superior advantages in comfort and living. The new style of buildings here referred to retain their character of a flat, while they will give board in a dining room common to all the tenants.

There are no less than three such buildings under course of construction on the west side, while a well-known Broadway flat is being turned into a building similar in kind. The last is the "Saratoga" or "Sidney," on the northwest corner of Broadway and 53rd street. The owners of this flat felt that they could rent their suites to better advantage if they turned the building into a hotel. The others are the two Brennan buildings on Central Park West, between 74th and 75th streets, and the Hotel Beresford on the corner of Manhattan square and Central Park West.

The writer called upon Michael Brennan to ascertain what prompted him to build a hotel instead of two flats, as he had originally intended. The object was to gather an idea as to the motives which builders had in putting up this class of structures, and to learn whether they would be likely to be successful. His answer shows that the regulations of the Board of Health were primarily responsible for his change of plan, while the success of similar hotels elsewhere was the secondary cause. He said: "According to the present law you can only build a flat 80 feet high, even though your building is absolutely fireproof. This is an absurd and inconsistent law. I deem that a man or woman's life is as precious to them in an apartment house as it is in a hotel, and there ought to be no discrimination made between one and the other, so long as either building is fireproof. I first filed plans for two seven-story apartment houses. They were to have been not over 80 feet high and absolutely fireproof. When I came to make up my final calculations I found, however, that I could not build a seven-story fire-proof building and compete with the rents of flats that were not fire-proof, owing to the larger cost. I resolved to overcome this difficulty by adding two more stories, making them nine stories high, thus obtaining a sufficiently larger rental to cover the greater cost. The Building Department would have allowed me to build nine stories, as my plans called for heavy walls, regular warehouse walls, and for fire-proofing. The Health Department, however, objected, stating that I must determine upon the character of the building first. I then changed my plans to make the buildings apartment hotels, with one dining room for all the tenants. I got the idea from seeing how successful one or two other of these hotels had been. People seem to be drifting into wishing to live in them. They are so much troubled with servants, while it costs less and saves considerable annoyance. The Winthrop, on 7th avenue and 124th and 125th streets, is an example of the success of the apartment hotel. The Saratoga, on Broadway and 53d street has been turned into a similar building, while I have heard it said that the Clark estate have discussed the advisability of doing the same thing with the Dakota."

The writer then called at the Hotel Beresford, and saw the owner, A.S. Walker. He said: "The Winthrop, which I built, is an example of the remarkable success of the apartment hotel. It is not only full all the time, but we have a thousand applicants every year for rooms. The Beresford is now half rented, though the building will not be finished until October 1. The success of the apartment hotel depends upon three things: 1. The location. 2. The interior plans. 3. It must be run properly. It must be on a corner and near the Elevated road station; it must be planned so as to make things convenient for the tenants, and it must be conducted, both in the service and table, so as to give satisfaction. Capitalists are not likely, for that very reason, to invest freely in them, because they will be afraid of the management not proving successful. The owners will in most cases have to run the buildings themselves or lease them."

The apartment hotel has come into existence owing to the desire on the part of many people to get rid of the cares and expenses of housekeeping, especially in the matter of servants. They simply rent their suite of rooms, including chamber service, and pay so much per capita for board. This is the main feature in which the apartment hotel differs from the ordinary hotel, where the charge includes both room and board.

FIG. 148   The Hotel San Remo, circa 1893, with the north façade of the Dakota beyond. The site of the Langham to the left of the San Remo is still a vacant lot, as is the site of the Kenilworth to the right. *Courtesy of the Office for Metropolitan History.*

# APPENDIX H

T<small>HIS</small> <small>ARTICLE</small> was published in the 9 October 1880 edition of the *Real Estate Record & Guide*.

## THE MAMMOTH FAMILY HOTEL.

**T**wo years, at least, will be required for the completion of the grand family hotel for which the foundations have just been laid on the Eighth avenue, between Seventy-second and Seventy-third streets. The situation is, indeed, unsurpassed, it being high ground facing Central Park, and on the broad street forming the great connecting link with Riverside Park.

Of course, it is well known that Mr. Edward Clark, President of the Singer Manufacturing Company, and a large holder of West Side real estate, is to carry out this enterprise. He has a double object in erecting this extensive building, namely, to give an impetus to the improvement of the West Side, as well as to define the character of the buildings which should grace it, and to offer the city such an hotel as it is now greatly in need of, where persons of means can find a home equal in all its comforts and luxuries to our first class private dwellings, surpassing them in location and without their entailed discomforts and inconveniences; in short, such a place of residence as can be found in some of the capitals of Europe, where persons of the highest rank occupy the different classes of similar family hotels, and live in great elegance.

In this country the conditions of living are different from those of all other countries except England, requiring the appointments of such an hotel to be superior to those of like buildings abroad, and it is the intention to make this one more complete in every detail of comfort, luxury and elegance than any yet erected.

The building has been designed by Mr. H. J. Hardenbergh, and will be erected under his supervision. It will be nine stories in height above the basement, will occupy the whole frontage of 204 feet of the block on Eighth avenue, and present a front of 200 feet on each of the streets named. The style will be Renaissance, of the period of Francis 1st. The materials of the fronts will be Nova Scotia stone and fine pressed brick, the former profusely used, handsomely moulded and carved. In plan the building encloses a large court, the pavement of which is on a level with the street and having an opening on the north side extending from the pavement to the roof line.

The main entrance in on the south (or Seventy- second street) front, through a broad, open arched driveway into the court, in the four angles of which are the entrances and stairways to the different suites of apartments. The rooms for the porter or *concierge* open on this passage and command a view at all times. On the north front is a second or inferior entrance for persons on foot only. On the west side of the building will be a driveway running through from street to street, and this will be inclined to the level of the basement floor and be for the service of the building and of the tradespeople. Under the main court will be a second court reached by the driveway just named, where all the working of the great house may take place unseen.

There will be between forty and fifty suites of apartments, of sizes varying from five to twenty rooms, all of large proportions. On the main floor, fronting Eighth avenue and Seventy-second street will be a fine restaurant comprising main dining hall, café, and private dining rooms. This will have an entrance from the street direct, and will offer accommodations to transient visitors as well as to persons living in the house. Many of the suites will be arranged with kitchens attached, others with dining rooms only, so that it may be optional with tenants whether they are served from the restaurant or not.

The basement will be devoted to kitchens, engine rooms, janitors apartments and private storage rooms; the attics to servants rooms and laundries.

The building will be entirely fireproof in every part and constructed in the most thorough manner. Seven large hydraulic elevators will run to different floors and as many staircases of iron and marble will be placed in different parts of the buildings.

The woodwork throughout will be of the finest varieties in use, in many cases elaborately finished. The building will cost over a million dollars.

# APPENDIX I

I N ITS ISSUE for 10 September 1884, *The Daily Graphic* published this article, accompanied by a floor plan and artist's rendering of the building.

## THE DAKOTA.

### A DESCRIPTION OF ONE OF THE MOST PERFECT APARTMENT HOUSES IN THE WORLD.

Probably not one stranger out of fifty who ride over the elevated roads or on either of the rivers does not ask the name of the stately building which stands west of Central Park, between Seventy-second and Seventy-third streets. If there is such a person the chances are that he is blind or nearsighted. The name of the building is the Dakota Apartment House, and it is the largest, most substantial, and most conveniently arranged apartment house of the sort in this country. It stands on the crest of the West Side Plateau, on the highest portion of land in the city, and overlooks the entire island and the surrounding country.

From the east one has a bird's-eye view of Central Park. The reservoir castle and the picturesque lake, the museums, and the mall are all shown at a glance. From this point also can be seen Long Island Sound in the distance, and the hills of Brooklyn.

From the north one looks down on High Bridge and the tall reservoir tower, which looks as slender as a needle.

From the west can be seen the Palisades, the Orange Mountains, and the broad Hudson, which narrows into a silver thread as the double row of hills close together far away in the distance.

Looking south one sees the tall towers of Brooklyn Bridge, Governor's Island, and far beyond the green hills of Staten Island and the blue waters of the Lower Bay.

Every prominent landmark in the landscape can be distinguished from this location, and the great buildings of the lower city are as prominently marked as if the sightseer were floating over the island in a balloon. At this elevation every breeze which moves across Manhattan from any direction is felt. This is a feature which needs no emphasis to make attractive such stifling days as these.

The building is of the Renaissance style of architecture, built of buff brick, with carved Nova Scotia freestone trimmings and terra cotta ornamentation. Although there is a profusion of ornament in the shape of bay and octagon windows, niches, balconies, and balustrades, with spandrels and panels in beautiful terra cotta work and heavily carved cornices, the size and massive construction of the edifice prevent any appearance of superfluity.

The building is about 200 feet square and 10 stories high, the upper two stories being in the handsome mansard roof which, with its peaks and gables, surmounted by ornate copper work cresting and finials, and relieved by dormer and oriel windows, gives the entire structure an air of lightness and elegance.

The construction is of the most massive character, and the aim of the owners has been to produce a building monumental in solidity and perfectly fireproof.

The brick and mason work is of unusual weight, the walls being in some places four feet thick, and the partitions and flooring have iron beams and framing, filled in with concrete and fireproof material.

On the Seventy-third-street side there is a handsome doorway, and on the Seventy-second-street front a fine arched carriage entrance, with groined roof and elegant stone carving. Both entrances lead into the inner court, from which four separate passages afford access to the interior of the building.

From the ground floor four fine bronze staircases, the metal work beautifully wrought and the walls wainscoted in rare marbles and choice hard woods, and four luxuriously fitted elevators, of the latest and safest construction, afford means of reaching the upper floors.

The ladies' sitting room, adjoining the staircase in the southeast corner, will be decorated by the Misses Greatorex, a guarantee that the work upon it will be artistic and unconventional.

There are four iron staircases and four elevators enclosed in massive brick walls and extending from the cellar to the kitchens and servants' quarters in the upper stories, separate from the rest of the house, which can be used for domestic purposes, carrying furniture, merchandise, &c. There are electric bells to each elevator, and a complete system of electric communication throughout the house.

The building is in four great divisions, which enclose a courtyard as large as half a dozen ordinary buildings. This gives every room in the house light, sunshine, and ventilation.

Under this courtyard is the basement, into which lead broad entrances for the use of tradesmen's teams. Here are situated the most interesting portions of the building, or at least the most novel ones. The floor is of asphaltum, as dry and hard as rock. This basement, also, has a courtyard as large as the one above, and lighted by two huge latticed manholes, which look like a couple of green flower beds in the stone flooring. Off of this yard are the storerooms of the house, in which the management will store the furniture and trunks of the tenants free of charge. A porter is assigned to this duty alone. The rooms are all marble floored, lighted and heated, and accessible at all hours of the day or night. The rooms of the servants are also on this floor. These consist of separate dining and toilet rooms for the male and female servants and a male reading and smoking room. These are not for the personal servants of the tenants, but for the general help of the management, which will not number far from 150 persons.

The laundry, kitchen, pantry, and bake shops, and private storerooms are here also, for the owners combine a hotel with the apartment house, and furnish eating facilities for all the tenants of the building who prefer it on the table d'hôte plan.

Opening from the lower court, and extending under the open ground in the rear of the building, a large vault, 150 feet long, 60 feet wide, and 18 feet deep, is now being excavated. When finished it will contain the steam boilers, steam engines, &c., for hoisting, pumping, &c., and the dynamos for supplying electric illumination in the Dakota and adjoining 27 houses. The vault will be roofed with iron beams and brick filling arches and made flush with the land in the rear of the building, 225 feet deep, which will be laid out as a garden. The boilers, with the furnaces, machinery, &c., will thus be located outside the walls of the building safely remote.

The first floor contains the dining rooms, which are finished in a perfect manner. In this case these words really mean something. The floors are of marble and inlaid. The base of the walls is of English quartered oak, carved by hand. The upper portions are finished in bronze bas-relief work, and the ceilings are also quartered oak, beautifully carved. The effect is that of an old English baronial hall, with the dingy massiveness brightened and freshened without losing any of its richness. The effect is heightened by a large Scotch brownstone engraved fireplace, which ornaments the centre of the room.

The business office has oral communication with every portion of the house, and the wants of the tenants can be attended to as quickly as can be done by human ingenuity and a perfectly arranged service.

In addition to the four staircases mentioned before, which are finished in bronze and marble, there are four iron staircases for servants, four passenger elevators, and four servants' elevators.

The Dakota will be divided into 65 different suites of apartments, each containing from four to twenty separate rooms, so that accommodations can be furnished either for bachelors or for large families.

There is an air of grandeur and elegance not only about the halls and stairways but also about the separate apartments that cannot probably be found in any other house of this kind in the country.

The parlors in some instances are 25 by 40 feet, with other rooms in proportion, and there are in many cases private halls to the suites, furnished with fine bronze mantels, tiled hearths, and ornamental open fireplaces.

The parlors, libraries, reception and dining rooms are all cabinet trimmed, paneled, and wainscoted in mahogany, oak, and other attractive and durable woods, and are furnished with carved buffets and mantels, mirrors, tiled hearths and open grate fireplaces, and parqueted floors.

The kitchens are spacious, and provided with ranges, with ventilation hoods, all with Minton tiled facing and marble wainscoting. There are porcelain washtubs, large storerooms and closets, and butlers' pantries, equipped in the most complete manner, and each suite has its private bathrooms and closets, fitted with the most approved scientific sanitary appliances.

The plumbing and hygienic arrangements are fully equal to anything in this country. On the top story are six tanks, holding 5,000 gallons of water each, and supplied by steam pumps having a daily capacity of 2,000,000 gallons, and about 200 miles of pipe have been used in effecting its circulation. Not only in the sanitary appliances, but in every other department, there is a completeness that is surprising. the precautions taken to secure proper ventilation and a pure atmosphere, to insure safety to occupants in cases of fire or panic, and to extinguish fire are perfect.

When opened, the comfort and convenience of the guests will be further insured by the accommodations of the dining rooms, laundry, and barber's shop, run to the most improved plan, in connection with the building. It is the perfection of the apartment style of living, and guarantees to the tenants comforts which would require unlimited wealth to procure in a private residence. The wisest precautions have been taken to insure freedom from the ordinary cares of the household to the fortunate tenants.

For instance, the coal and kindling wood are purchased by the manager in large quantities and sold to the tenants, who take in exchange for their money tickets which are presented at the office, and the fuel is carried to their rooms in convenient quantities, thereby saving the user from any of the necessary troubles in buying and storage. This may seem like a small matter, but it is only one of the hundred plans taken by the owners to secure the comfort of the tenants.

It is almost needless to state that the building is as nearly fireproof as any which can be erected. There are continuous passageways extending through the four divisions on the roof; ninth, eighth, and first stories.

On the tenth floor there is provision for a play room and gymnasium for the children, well lighted and ventilated and commanding a grand view of the city and surroundings, while on the ninth floor there will be extra servants' rooms, private laundries and drying rooms, dormitories for transient male and female servants and attachés of the building, and lavatories, toilet rooms, and bathrooms for their use.

The work on both the Dakota and the neighboring apartment house and private dwellings owned by the estate has been done not only in the most careful manner, but with a view to permanence and convenience, and to symmetry as well as beauty of appearance. The greatest skill and experience and the best materials large means could command have been employed, and the manner in which the work in each department has been done reflects the greatest credit on those intrusted with it, especially upon the architect, Mr. H.J. Hardenbergh, who has supervised the work from its commencement to its now rapidly approaching completion.

Both the Dakota, the private residences, and the smaller apartment house are now ready for occupation, and we need hardly comment on the peculiar attractions they will possess for those who have experienced a desire for an eligible residence on the west side.

The natural and artificial attributes of the position are all in favor of the buildings, which for comfort, ample space, salubrity, convenience, and accessibility cannot be excelled, and a glance at our description will suffice to show that everything skill could furnish, ingenuity and experience suggest has been supplied.

The managers of the Clark estate, the owners of the property, are well known for their fairness and liberality to tenants, and every care will be taken to insure comfort and wellbeing. The rents are moderate when compared with the accommodations furnished, and those desiring to secure either dwellings or apartments can examine plans, &c., and make arrangements at the office of the estate, at

No. 25 West Twenty-third-street, New York.

## APPENDIX J

O<small>N</small> 7 M<small>ARCH</small> 1885, the *Real Estate Record & Guide* published this detailed and laudatory report.

### THE DAKOTA APARTMENT HOUSE

W<small>E</small> present our readers to-day with a picture of this immense apartment house. The Dakota is one of the largest structures of the kind in the world. It may aptly be termed the "mammoth" apartment house, on account of its size and the area it covers. It is an imposing structure. It towers high and above every up town building on the west side, and viewed from an altitude is one of the principal objects for miles around. It over-looks the Central Park, and has a total frontage of 808 feet, 204 on Eighth avenue, 200 on Seventy-second, 200 on twenty-third street, and 204 to the westward, where, owing to the private park adjoining, its light will be unimpeded by structures opposite. In the matter of light, situation and dimension, the Dakota is unsurpassed by any apartment house in the city. Noble in appearance as is the exterior, it is necessary, in order to gain an approximate idea of the size, to explore the interior. Here, the visitor is lost, as it were, in immensity. Room after room is passed, until their numbers appear legion. The inside is approached through a carriage drive, with groined ceilings, leading to a large open court, 55x90, accessible to each of the eight entrances leading to the different floors of the build-ing. There are fifty-eight suites, containing eight to twenty rooms each, renting from $1,000 to $5,600 per annum, and there are six hundred and twenty-three rooms in all.

The largest in the building is the dining-room, and for its size, 25x95, the handsomest on Manhattan Island. The ceiling is in finely carved English quartered oak. The fireplac-es are quite a feature, being some fifteen feet high, and composed of a pleasant looking Scotch brown stone, doing special service for this purpose, while the tiling is in Mosaic. Standing at the end of the chamber and gaining a perspective an idea of its size is ob-tained, and should the guests of the Dakota ever feel disposed to have a ball, they will find ample space for dancing on the polished floors of this spacious apartment. Adjoining is a private dining-room for the accommodation of the guests should any of them desire to entertain their friends in privacy. The room is elegantly fitted up in mahogany, while the wall covering is of a fireproofing material of handsome design in imitation of majolica. A large beveled glass window appears to the west, and when lit up produces a fine effect. We now turn into the ladies' reception room. This is the gem of the house; not in size, be it said, but in richness of adornment. It forms an exception to every other room in the building, in so far as the work is the art of feminine hands. Nine curtains adorn the cham-ber. Five of these are of satin, covered with elegantly painted flowers and leaves in oil, the remainder being of dark green plush velvet, the furniture covering to match. The frieze is beautifully decorated with clematis, the tendrils leaning over gracefully towards the door. The handiwork of this room is wholly that of the sisters Greatorex, with the excep-tion of the clever etchings on the walls, which were drawn by the mother of those ladies.

We now ascend one of the four grand staircases leading to the upper portion of the building. The wainscoting is of the choicest marbles, each panel being of different color and design. A broad strip of Mexican onyx surmounts the whole, and forms a striking re-lief to the more somber tints by which it is surrounded. The balusters from top to bottom are of a pretty design in iron, and resting here awhile we peer up into the heights to catch a glimpse of the tenth story. We now ascend one of the handsome elevators and step out opposite one of the largest suites in the house. The drawing room is approached through a vestibule some twelve feet square, containing a well designed and finely wrought grate and mantel in iron. This chamber is 24x30 in dimension. The trim is of mahogany, and the floor parqueted. It contains a very handsome chandelier of unique design in brass, with appliances for gas or electricity, exclusive of four additional brackets of similar de-sign in different parts of the room, which contains altogether some forty electric lights. Adjoining, entered through massive sliding doors, is a reception room, 18x20, in mahog-any, with elegant mantels; and beyond this is a library, 19x24, fitted up similarly. Then comes a ladies' boudoir, 15x27. To describe each chamber in the suite would occupy too much space, but suffice it to say that in addition to these rooms there is a large dining-room, 18x24, carved in oak, directly opposite the drawing-room, and beyond the library are no less than nine bedrooms, varying in size from 14x23 to 22x23, bathrooms, toilet, dressing and billiard rooms, servants' apartments, butler's pantry – in fact, twenty rooms in all.

A glance at some of the other suites displays similar elegance and size, though many are of more modest pretensions, containing half the number of rooms of that described. One of the features of the building is the great length of the halls, from which access is gained to each room. It is quite a little promenade to traverse them from end to end. They are 170 feet in length on each floor and 5 feet in width. We now ring the bell for the elevator and ascend to one or the highest altitudes on Manhattan Island.

Once on the roof, a splendid view meets the eye. Being a clear day we can see 36 miles westward, 25 to the northeast, and 20 to the south. In the distance the Orange Mountains are seen, at our feet are the Hudson River and the Palisades: the bay, with Staten Island in the distance, looms up before us, while high bridge, the Obelisk, and Hell Gate are on the one side, and huge apartment houses and other buildings appear towards the south, flanked by the Brooklyn Bridge. But the prettiest sight of all—one well worth seeing last week – was the thousands of skaters on the Central Park lakes moving to and fro, looking like Lilliputians from that great height, while the hundreds of sleighs with their tinkling bells, the long string of carriages and other vehicles, combined with the general surroundings, made the scene most picturesque.

Turning from this feast of the sight, we proceed to examine the roof of the building, which is quite a little hamlet in itself. It is all copper-plated, with the exception of the gables, which are tiled in slate. Twelve large tanks are situated on different corners. Portions of the roof, those for instance over-looking the Central Park and the Palisades, would make an excellent retreat in summer time from the heat indoors, owing to the refreshing breeze, which forever blows at such an altitude.

Having explored the heights, a peep into the depths may not be uninteresting. One touch of the electric bell and an elevator comes sailing up at our beckon call and we descend into the lower regions of the Dakota. We commence by entering the boiler room. Here are eight tubular boilers supplying steam power for the building, and we found workmen engaged continually shoveling coal into the furnaces. The engineer on being asked how munch coal had been used during the preceding twenty four hours replied, "twenty-two tons." The most interesting room is that containing the electrical apparatus. The dynamos have a capacity of 120-horse power. The whole is under the care and supervision of an expert electrician, and as dusk was drawing nigh we were just in time to witness the machinery commence to work preparatory to conducting the light to the building.

The writer was accompanied by a representative of the Clark estate and by Mr. Chatterton, the courteous manager, who very intelligently answered all queries addressed to him. Passing by the large laundry and ironing room, 25x80, we came upon the pump roam, size 22x60, where we saw the machinery in operation having a capacity of 2,000,000 gallons per diem. Then comes a store room, bakery, pastry-room, dish room, larder-room, and the kitchen, 25x70, from which a ventilator, eight feet in diameter, runs to the top of the building. There are various other rooms for the use of servants, and we must not forget the barber shop, where we peeped in to see some of the guests being submitted to the tender mercies of the tonsorial artist.

Ascending to the office on the first floor, an immense number of electric bells and speaking tubes meet the eye. These give the manager control of all the employees in the building from that spot, and enables him to communicate with every corner of the structure. The writer asked for an example of the efficiency of the system, and it was at once practically demonstrated to him. The bell was pressed communicating with the man running the eastern elevator. The signal was immediately returned. A question was put to him through the speaking tube communicating with him, and his reply came back at once in clear and audible tones. It was but the work of half a minute.

Speaking of the electric light, which is in every room of the building, it may be added that 4,000 electric lights are distributed throughout the Dakota and 300 electric bells. There are special private wires communicating with all the fire stations, together with a telegraphic instrument enabling an operator to converse with the various fire stations, and also wires to the Dakota stables, telegraph and messenger offices, florist, etc.

The building is in hard-wood trim and contains steam heat throughout. The chandeliers all over the house are of elegant design and have alone cost many tens of thousands of dollars.

The plumbing is of a sanitary character and the ventilation and light is unsurpassed. The building contains four passenger, and four servants and freight elevators.

The Dakota is estimated to have cost between $1,500,00 and 2,000,000. It is thoroughly fireproof—that is, as fireproof as human ingenuity could possibly make it—and this has been recognized by the fire insurance companies, who have rated it at from fifteen to forty cents for three years. Though free from mortgage, the taxes, assessments and running expenses will amount to about $50,000 per annum when fully occupied, though a large number of suites are still to rent. The arrangements in every part of the structure are perfect, and every possible accommodation that can minister to the comfort and happiness of human beings is provided, regardless of labor and cost.

To describe in detail all the features of this immense structure would be impossible in the limited space at our command, but the above sketch will give the reader some idea of one of the noblest apartment houses in the world.

ANDREW ALPERN has written four other books about New York apartment buildings: *The New York Apartment Houses of Rosario Candela and James Carpenter*; *Luxury Apartment Houses of Manhattan*; *Historic Manhattan Apartment Houses*; and *Apartments for the Affluent* (reprinted as *New York's Fabulous Luxury Apartment Houses*). He is co-author with real estate developer Seymour Durst of *HOLDOUTS! The Buildings That Got In The Way*; and he has written three additional books about law and architecture, plus a catalogue of his collection of drawing instruments at the Avery Architectural Library at Columbia University. He is an architectural historian, an architect, and an attorney at law.

CHRISTOPHER S. GRAY is an architectural historian who wrote the weekly Streetscapes column in the Sunday real estate section of *The New York Times* for more than 25 years. He has also published two anthologies of his columns: *New York Streetscapes, Tales of Manhattan's Significant Buildings and Landmarks*; and *Changing New York, The Architectural Scene*. In addition, he is the author of *Blueprints, Twenty-Six Extraordinary Structures*; and *New York at Night*; and he has edited or contributed to: *Fifth Avenue 1911 From Start To Finish*; *Building New York*; *New York Empire City 1920-1945*; *The Chrysler Building, Creating a New York Icon*; and *New York* by Reinhardt Wolf. He has also published many magazine articles and for forty years has operated the Office for Metropolitan History, a research organization serving the community of scholars and real estate professionals in New York.

KENNETH G. GRANT is a retired travel industry journalist and web producer/programmer who records New York's architectural environment and employs technology to capture and enhance the city's memorable buildings.
His work can been seen at www.NewYorkitecture.com

# INDEX

Where a page reference is in **bold**, it signifies an illustration or the caption to one.

*Set in Miller, Bell, & Scotch types.*
*Printed on Phoenixmotion Xantur paper*
*by the Covington Group. Designed by*
*Jerry Kelly, New York.*

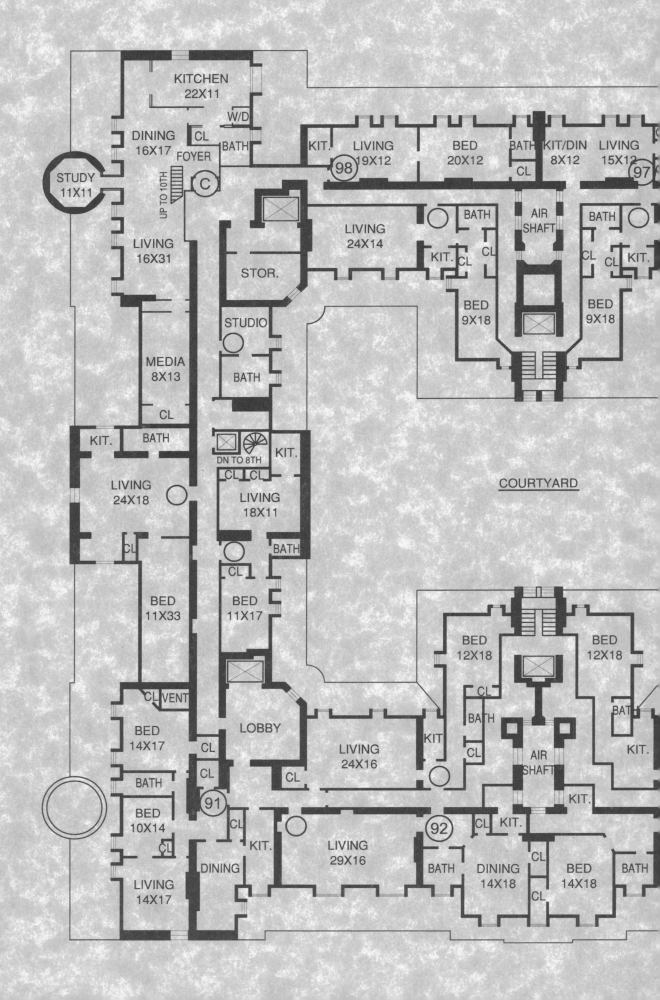